Journeys with Kids

America's Desertlands with kids

PKS Media
Canmore, Alberta
Canada

T*he Mission of Journeys with Kids Books/PKS Media Inc. is to serve our clients, customers, families and friends by publishing practical, fun and important information that encourages exploration and memorable family* experiences.

Edited by Tom Winterhoff and Lyle Jenish, QJE Publishing and Creative
Art Direction by Lyle Jenish and Jacqueline Rimmer, QJE Publishing and Creative
Cover and text design by Lyle Jenish and Jacqueline Rimmer, QJE Publishing and Creative
Photography by Philip & Karen Smith, PKS Media Inc.
Illustrations by Florence Regehr, Karen Smith and Julia Smith

Copyright © 2006 PKS Media Inc.

Published by
Journeys with Kids Books/PKS Media Inc.
10 Blue Grouse Ridge, Canmore,
Alberta T1W 1L5 Canada

Although we've endeavored to provide factual information insofar as possible within this guide, the authors and Journeys with Kids accept no responsibility for issues arising from wrong or misleading facts or points of view.

Backcountry activities – such as, but not limited to, climbing, mountain biking, hiking, desert trekking, skiing and camping – are inherently dangerous. As such, we cannot accept responsibility for injury or loss to persons following the suggestions of this guide, or in any other way using it.

Printed and bound in Canada by Friesens, One Printers Way, Altona, Manitoba

National Library of Canada Cataloguing in Publication Data

Smith, Philip
Regehr, Scott
America's Desertlands with kids: journeys with kids

ISBN 0-9738947-1-7

Visit our website at www.journeyswithkids.com

TABLE OF CONTENTS

Acknowledgements IV
Preface V
About the authors VII
Introduction IX

Chapter 1: Joshua Tree National Park   14
Chapter 2: Eastern Sierra   24
Chapter 3: Death Valley National Park   34
Chapter 4: Zion National Park   40
Chapter 5: Bryce Canyon National Park To Capital Reef National Park   50
Chapter 6: Lake Powell   61
Chapter 7: Moab   65
Chapter 8: Arches National Park & Canyonlands National Park   75
Chapter 9: MesaVerde National Park   85
Chapter 10: Navaho Nation   91
Chapter 11: Grand Canyon National Park and Petrified Forest National Park   100
Chapter 12: Sedona   106
Chapter 13: Organ Pipe Cactus National Monument   113
Chapter 14: Tuscon   121
Chapter 14: New Mexico and Western Texas   130
Chapter 15: Southwest Highways   143
Chapter 16: Kid's Stuff   157
Travel Essentials   167
Glossary   183
Appendix   184
Future titles   190

ACKNOWLEDGEMENTS

First and foremost, we'd like to thank the youngest members of the JWK project – Joshua and Julia – for their endless enthusiasm to explore and discover new places, activities, and things, along with us. Thanks to their mom, Karen, for contributing photographically and in numerous other ways. Many thanks to all of those others, both kids and adults, who've joined us on our mountain forays.

Thanks to Graham Twomey for contributing maps, creative ideas and computer expertise. Thanks also to Lyle Jenish and his crew for helping to take this project from bits and pieces to fruition. Thanks to Florence Regehr for her encouragement and loving care of our kids at pivotal moments. Finally, a special thanks to all of you who've supported the creation of this guide and suggested ways to make it especially relevant for adventuresome families.

PREFACE

Traveling through the Southwest while preparing this edition of Journeys with Kids was more than just great fun and full of rich experiences; it was also incredibly educational for all of us. We explored this region extensively during our BC days (i.e. Before Children) and thought we knew it well. Kids, however, have the ability to put a new spin on every old experience. Some of their fireside questions ("Where did cliff-dwelling people go to the washroom?" or "Aren't there scorpions and black widow spiders in that piece of firewood you're holding?") remain pretty much unanswered years later.

Knowing exactly what to write about within these pages proved to be challenging. Across the vast spaces of the Southwest, there are literally thousands — and maybe millions — of exciting nooks and crannies that are worth investigating. Pinpointing the ones that warrant special attention (the destinations included in our "Activities" and "Itineraries" sections) meant we had to ignore many other great places and worthwhile rambles.

Our kids helped enormously with this undertaking. They served as the catalyst for our determination to

produce a guide that parents would find useful and entertaining, after we were unable to find any other travel literature that described safe but exciting routes for families to explore in the Southwest.

Just as importantly, Josh and Julia let us know in no uncertain terms (either with whoops of joy or groans of displeasure) whether the routes we trekked were "kid-friendly" or utterly lacking in juvenile appeal. This book is, in many ways, a summary of their sentiments.

Our experiences traveling in the Southwest — even during the occasional car breakdown — have always been good ones. Rarely is the sun not shining, and the people we've met along the way have generally been kind and generous. At times, our travels have been absolutely enchanting.

If this is your first visit to the Southwest, I hope you will also experience the region's unique magic. If you're returning for another visit or live in the area, then it's my sincere wish that this book will help you discover new and exciting paths.

Philip Smith

ABOUT THE AUTHORS

Philip Smith

As a widely acclaimed photographer, filmmaker and author of the book Mountain Photography (Heritage House), Philip has spent much of his career traveling to intriguing destinations around the world. One of his favorite places to explore is America's Desertlands, a place he's wandered through for months at a stretch with eyes wide open for new visual discoveries.

Philip grew up in the Canadian Rocky Mountains, an environment somewhat analogous to the Southwest (albeit colder). He spent his formative years gaining an appreciation of rugged wilderness areas and developing his survival skills, and has since trekked or skied along the challenging mountain spines of the Rockies, Alaska's St. Elias and South America's Andes Mountains. Philip has hiked and biked thousands of kilometres of wilderness trails and climbed hundreds of summits — including several "first ascents" along the way.

He feels incredibly fortunate to now share his outdoor experiences with his kids Joshua and Julia, and his wife Karen. They often return to some of the same hangouts that Philip discovered as a kid. When not traveling to exotic locales or planning a family trip to some far-flung part of the globe, the family might be found stringing a Tyrolean traverse in a front yard that overlooks snow-capped mountains or teaching the kids next door the delicate art of rappelling from a nearby treehouse.

Scott Regehr

As the intrepid uncle of the Smith kids and a long-time broadcast journalist with the Canadian Broadcasting Corporation (CBC), Scott chose to take notes for this travel guide at intriguing moments: just as the nose of our whitewater raft dipped beneath the waves near Moab or from his rear end on a mountain bike trail near

Bishop. Scott had fallen off his bike and his 12-year-old nephew Joshua whizzed by him, overhead.

For Scott, this is typical stuff. During his career with the CBC, he has written stories from an igloo in the high Arctic while the temperature (including the wind chill) dropped to -60 Fahrenheit outside; alongside an aircraft suspected of being hijacked on September 11, 2001; and at the end of an 800-kilometre walk along the famous Spanish pilgrimage route, the Camino de Santiago.

When the opportunity arose to research and write about the American Southwest, one of his favorite regions of the world, he jumped in with both feet. Like when he was researching and writing television or radio documentaries for the CBC, Scott's contribution to America's Desertlands with Kids included many hours spent inside an office, making phone calls and pecking away at the computer. But unlike working with Canada's national broadcaster, his field research this time involved tagging along behind the Smith kids and their friends. Really. He has tire marks on his legs to prove it.

American Southwest

The region known as the American Southwest inspired the Bugs Bunny-Roadrunner Hour, The Flintstones and the Saturday cowboy matinees that many of us grew up watching on television — the same episodes our kids still enjoy today. There is a very good reason for that; the American Southwest landscape is stunningly dramatic and encompasses the romance of an old-fashioned western as well as the exaggerated vividness of a cartoon.

Southwest Arizona's cacti can grow up to two storeys tall and congregate around sandstone pillars that soar to the height of 200 storeys. Almost everything there is larger than the imagination can envision. Now just imagine what the Grand Canyon looks like through a child's eyes!

Approximately the same size as Western Europe, America's Southwest has the highest concentration of national parks on the U.S. mainland. The area's history is just as grand as its skyline. Illustrated in tintype photographs, scorched by gunpowder and delineated by railroads and barbed wire, it is also controversial and spiced up with legends, lore and the exploits of larger-than-life personalities such as Kit Carson, Butch Cassidy, Wyatt Earp, Geronimo and Sitting Bull.

The Southwest is an enormous "living classroom". Dusted with vibrant desert colours of orange, purple and red, the otherworldly landscape raises many questions: How have Mesa Verde National Park's 700-year-old cliff dwellings remained perfectly intact? How do natural stone arches form? How did Tombstone, Arizona get its name?

Seek out ancient petroglyphs and explore ghost towns with your children. Embark on a river rafting or rock climbing adventure, go horseback riding, rent a houseboat or check out some of the fabulous hikes and bike rides the Southwest has to offer.

Our hope is that our recommended itineraries and activities inspire you and your family

to explore America's fascinating Southwest landscape. Don't feel constrained by our suggestions, however. In many ways, this book only scratches the surface of the great Southwest adventure. Use our routes as guides — and then feel free to deviate from them if the urge takes you.

We've organized the book's chapters geographically, roughly from west to east, for no real reason except convenience. (New Mexico is every bit as worthy a place to visit as eastern California!). How you use the book will depend on where your travel adventures begin and end, or on what part of the Southwest you choose to focus on.

The starting points ("Bases") detailed in this book were chosen with the following questions in mind: Is there a wide range of accommodation available? Is there access to a grocery store? Is there a good selection of places to eat? Are there attractions that will be of interest to families when they're not out on the trails? Are there adequate medical services nearby? Can each destination be made to feel like a "home away from home"?

We have hiked, climbed or biked our way through every itinerary in this book, mostly with our kids. We have included distances, estimated travel times and difficulty ratings

for all of the routes. Itineraries rated as "easy" can be handled by physically fit kids aged five and up. Itineraries listed as "moderate" are suitable for fit kids over seven years of age. Anything listed as "difficult" is appropriate for fit kids aged 10 and up.

There will inevitably be days on any trip when the kids (and maybe mom and dad, too) will want to take a break from hiking or walking the trails. The "Activities in the Area" sections include a good mix of the best cultural, educational, sporting and entertainment options available nearby.

We've endeavored to highlight worthwhile driving routes (in our "Southwest Highways" chapter) that might not always be obvious, especially for travelers visiting the area for the first time. We've also suggested ways to make the most of a limited amount of holiday time, in order to maximize everyone's enjoyment, while at the same time steering clear of travel "burnout".

Our "Travel Essentials" chapter includes important information to help the whole family enjoy a smooth trip. We recommend reading it thoroughly before setting out, especially the sections on "Packing Your Bags" and "Getting There". The "Health and Safety" section contains tips to help keep your activities as safe as possible, whether you're in the midst of the Southwest's wildest regions or enjoying one of its luxurious spas.

The "Kids' Stuff" chapter is intended to address many of the questions that kids may raise when first experiencing the unfamiliar Southwest environment. The

"Entertainment Ideas" section provides loads of games and fun pastimes to keep kids busy while on the road or relaxing in a hotel room.

We hope this guide offers a pleasing balance of inspiration and information to make your trip to America's Southwest an exciting, safe and rewarding experience. Happy trails!

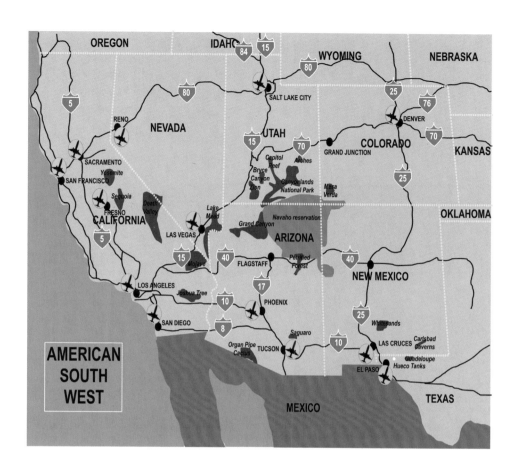

Joshua Tree National Park

The park is huge
– almost 800,000 acres
- and incredibly varied.

Joshua Tree National Park is loaded with funky natural shapes of all kinds

Our impressions of Joshua Tree National Park during our first trip there weren't exactly favorable. Yes, we did appreciate those funky-looking trees that dotted the landscape and it looked like the granite boulders would be fun to climb on, but much of the park appeared to be drab and boring.

With each successive visit, however, our feelings about the place have changed for the better. It's now one of our favorite destinations in the Southwest. That's not just because it's close to Los Angeles, which we travel to frequently, although it helps. Joshua Tree National Park is special in a way that eludes easy description.

You really have to camp out in the park for a night to fully experience its magic and appreciate its best features. It's an amazing place for a variety of activities, including hiking, camping, rock climbing and viewing wildlife. At times, it may seem like you are the only people in the park — so much so that you have to pinch yourself to remember that LA is just three hours away by car!

American Southwest

some of which just beg to be climbed

At almost 800,000 acres, the park is huge and incredibly varied. Summer temperatures are often brutally hot, but it also sometimes snows in the winter. The flora and fauna are similarly diverse. The creosote bush, ocotillo and cholla cactus contrast with the famous Joshua trees and fan palms in six oases around the park. Bighorn sheep, coyotes and golden eagles join lizards, snakes and countless bugs under the brilliant blue sky of the desert environment.

Native people traveled extensively through this area over many millennia, while harvesting pinyon nuts, mesquite beans, acorns and cactus fruit. It's believed that the Mojave Desert was much more lush in ancient times than it is now. The original inhabitants left behind rock paintings and fragments of pottery that were later discovered by non-native explorers, mainly cattle ranchers and gold miners of the late 19th century.

In turn, those people left behind reminders of the time they spent in the area. Joshua Tree's Lost Horse mine, Desert Queen mine and Key Ranch owe much to the tenacity and fortitude of these men and women, as well as the homesteaders who carried on their legacy in the 1930s.

Joshua Tree became a national park in 1994. Up to that point, it only had National Monument status. It's gradually become renowned worldwide as a winter rock climbing destination, boasting thousands of established routes and the potential for many more.

If you or your kids rock climb, you'll instantly appreciate Joshua Tree National Park. Even if you don't, we're sure you'll find lots of interesting pursuits to make your time here memorable. We've endeavored to summarize some of the better activities in the section below.

Biking and in-line skating

Joshua Tree's paved roads are great for both biking and in-line skating. Traffic is generally pretty sparse and slow-moving, the pavement is in pretty good condition and the grades are reasonable through the center of the park. Wearing a helmet and carrying adequate supplies of water are, of course, always recommended. So is taking along a map, just in case you become disoriented.

At present, biking is only allowed in the park on those roads that are also open to vehicles. This may soon change, since the park's new Backcountry and Wilderness Management Plan has designated about 29 miles of trails for non-motorized bike use. Until the U.S. Congress approves the plan, however, bikers cannot use those trails. Any change to this policy is probably 5 to 10 years off.

Climbing Headstone Rock

Headstone Rock, located beside the Ryan Campground, is one of the largest and most spectacular rocks in Joshua Tree National Park. There are a couple of excellent, moderate climbing routes running up it that kids with some climbing experience should be able to handle fairly easily. (The routes are rated from 5.6 to 5.9 on the American standard scale.) Rope, harnesses, good shoes and a few quick-draws are the only pieces of climbing gear you should need, along with at least one long sling for the top anchors.

You'll have no trouble spotting Headstone Rock from the Ryan campground if you look to the northeast. If you're not staying there, park in the gravel area near the entry point to the campground. (You'll have to circle through it first.)

Access to the climbing routes is at the west base of Headstone Rock on top of a jumble

Joshua Tree's roads are perfect for biking and skating

Headstone Rock is easy to spot from the Ryan campground

of boulders. Scramble up them from either the north or south side, but be careful; a fall between the boulders could be an ankle-buster — or worse!

The routes are graded as follows: the left-hand route (running along an exposed ridge crest) is rated 5.6, the middle route is rated 5.9 and the right-hand route (with excellent flakes) is rated 5.8. Note that you must top rope the middle route after climbing one of the others, owing to a lack of bolts.

Oases hikes

Either the 49 Palms Oasis hike or the Lost Palm Oasis hike will give you and your kids a first-hand look at a desert oasis and the very interesting fan palm, which requires a level of moisture not found in the park outside of the oases. The 49 Palms Oasis route starts from the extreme northern edge

Clean flakes on Headstone Rock

The view from Keys Point, looking southwest

of the park near the town of Twentynine Palms. The Lost Palm Oasis route begins at Cottonwood Oasis, near the park's southeast boundary.

The Lost Palm Oasis hike is more than double the length of the 49 Palms Oasis route — eight miles (return) vs. three miles. Depending on the amount of time you have available and the prevailing weather conditions, one route might make more sense than the other.

For these hikes and others, be sure to consult the map you receive when you enter the park, or else check with park personnel.

Joshua Tree Junior Ranger's Program

Once your kids have earned their Junior Ranger badges, they'll be able to tell you about the history of the area's original homesteaders, desert tortoises and Joshua trees. You can pick up the Junior Ranger workbook at the visitor center or in the ranger station at the park entrance.

The booklet encourages children to draw, write, attend a Ranger Program and pick up litter in the park. Kids aged 12 and under can participate and will receive a badge for their efforts.

For more information, call 760-367-5500 or check the website at www.nps.gov/jotr.

Joshua Tree Climbing School

More than 4,500 rock climbing routes have been established amongst the monzogranite formations in Joshua Tree National Park, so the park has become one of America's premier climbing destinations.

Joshua Tree/
Yucca Valley

If you or your kids have never climbed before, this school is just the ticket. Introductory courses are available for kids aged 10 and older. For families with younger children, private guides are available to show you the ropes.

For more information, call 1-800-890-4745 or check out the website at www.joshuatreerockclimbing.com.

as a

base

The communities of Joshua Tree and Yucca Valley (as well as Twentynine Palms, described below), are great bases for exploring Joshua Tree National Park. They all have numerous motels, service stations and food stores.

If you've been camping out in any of Joshua

Raven vs. Desert Tortoise

by Julia

If you're wandering through the Western Mojave Preserve in the spring, keep an eye out for desert tortoises. These creatures, which are nine to 15 inches long and have elephant-shaped legs, are most active during that time of the year.

"Active" may be overstating things a bit, since the tortoises spend 95 per cent of their lives in underground burrows! These incredible herbivores can survive for more than a year without water.

Despite this natural resilience, desert tortoise populations have dropped by 90 per cent since the 1980s — largely due to the local raven population. Juvenile tortoises are a favorite meal for these birds and biologists estimate that the big, black predators are responsible for least half of all tortoise deaths in the Mojave Desert.

If you hear a "hiss", "pop" or "poink" sound while hiking, there may be a desert tortoise in the immediate vicinity. Those are the sounds the tortoises make when they're distressed and the sounds are usually preceded by a raven's loud "Caww!"

Tree National Park's more "rustic" sites, a night or two spent in a motel will likely be much appreciated, as will a sit-down dinner at one of the restaurants found along the highway. Your park pass is good for multiple entries to the park within a one-week period (or 12-months, if you've bought a season pass), so don't worry about forfeiting your pass by leaving the park for a night or two. Be sure to keep your payment receipt if you leave the park, however, since it will be checked if you want to get back in.

Twentynine Palms

as a

base With a population of 28,000 people, Twentynine Palms is bigger than most of the "home bases" suggested in this book. But since the town is spread over nearly 54 square miles (about the size of San Francisco), we suspect your family won't feel too overwhelmed.

History has much to do with why the community covers such a large area. It's comprised of 160-acre homesteads that were originally offered to veterans returning from the First World War. Twentynine Palms was specifically chosen for the many soldiers who were recovering from mus-

Joshua Tree/ Yucca Valley

Travel times to:

Twentynine Palms: via Highway 62 (east); 30 minutes
Los Angeles: via Highway 62 (west), Highway 10 (west); 2 hours and 15 minutes
Palm Springs: via Highway 62 (west); 30 minutes

Josh embraces a Joshua Tree

tard gas poisoning, because of its moderate elevation (2,500 to 3,500 feet) and its clean, dry air. Today, descendants of those soldiers are counted among the town's inhabitants.

Twentynine Palms' military legacy lives on. The U.S. Marine Corps Air Ground Combat Center is located just north of the community. Spread over 932 square miles of desert, it is the largest Marine Corps base in the world.

What makes Twentynine Palms such a good base for families visiting the area? Well, it's situated close to two of America's most beautiful parks: Joshua Tree National Park and the Mojave National Preserve. This vibrant community is also ideal for families.

Pioneer Days festivities, which have been held every October since 1937, attract hundreds of visitors to the community each year. Outhouse races, parades, carnivals and chili cook-offs are all part of the fun. Most of the events are free to attend. Every December, the town puts on a Winter Lights Parade. Floats that have been decorated with hundreds of lights are paraded through the community, illuminating the desert night.

Because of its location on the cusp of the "Californian outback" and its proximity to a major military base, Twentynine Palms has a wide range of motels and hotels to choose from, including those of international motel chains. Joshua Tree National Park also has nine campgrounds within its boundaries.

Eateries range from Chinese and Mexican restaurants to standard pizza joints. Thanks to Joshua Tree's reputation within the international rock climbing community, there are also quite a few upscale and trendy restaurants to choose from.

Twentynine Palms

Travel times to:

Joshua Tree: via Highway 62 (west); 30 minutes
Los Angeles: via Highway 62 (west), Highway 10 (west); 2 hours and 45 minutes
Las Vegas: via Amboy Road (north), National Trails Highway (east), Highway 95 and Highway 93 (north); 4 hours and 45 minutes
Palm Springs: via Highway 62 (west); 1 hour
Death Valley: via Amboy Road (north), National Trail Highway (west), Highway 15 (north), Highway 127 (north), Highway 190 (north); 6 hours and 30 minutes

Twentynine Palms is probably the best place to stock up on groceries before heading out on a desert adventure. While you're getting your supplies, remember to budget for a minimum of one gallon of water per person per day to beat the desert heat.

Activities in the Twentynine Palms area:

Luckie Park

This park boasts a large outdoor swimming pool (open from Memorial Day to early September), two playground areas and a number of picnic shelters. If your kids are looking to burn off a little energy during the evening, check out the basketball courts, skateboard park, soccer field and four baseball fields.

To get to the park, drive to the intersection of Two Mile Road and Utah Trail.

For more information, call 760-367-6799.

Smith's Ranch Drive-In

For a town with such strong ties to the past, it's rather fitting that there's still a drive-in theatre here. For $3 per person (at the time this book was published), you can take in a double feature of the latest Hollywood fare underneath the stars.

The drive-in theatre is located at 4584 Adobe Rd.

For more information, call 760-367-7713.

Oasis of Murals

Spread throughout Twentynine Palms are 20 works of art painted on the sides of buildings. The large murals commemorate various aspects of the town's history and incorporate various themes, including city pioneers, local fauna and wildflowers, and Operation Iraqi Freedom. Although some of the murals seem a bit kitschy, your kids may get a kick out of trying to locate all 20 of them.

For more information, call 760-361-2286 or check out the website at www.oasisofmurals.com.

Mojave National Preserve

This expansive area of 1.4 million acres is the only National Park Service site where the Mojave Desert, the Great Basin Desert and the Sonoran Desert meet. It's a region where the plants, animals and geology are incredibly varied, so expect to see everything from sand dunes to mesas and extinct volcanoes.

At the Calico Early Man Site (on the shores of Lake Manix), primitive tools have been discovered that some scientists believe to be 200,000 years old.

Bagdad Cafe

Bagdad is a little town located on the outskirts of the Mojave National Preserve. You might remember seeing it in the 1980s cult film Bagdad Café.
Now a ghost town, Bagdad has an even more impressive distinction than fleeting Hollywood fame. This community once experienced the longest recorded period without rain of any community in the U.S.: a whopping 767 days between 1909 and 1912

To get a good look at cinder cones (remnants of volcanoes that were active 10,000 years ago), take a drive down Ailken's Mine Road. The road winds through about 30 of these formations.

At the Mitchell Caverns, you can visit the only limestone caves in the California State Park system. They consist of three caves filled with stalactites and stalagmites. Guided tours are 1½ hours long and are the only way to see the inside of the caverns. For more information, call 760-928-2586.

The Hole-in-the-Wall area is a popular spot for camping, hiking and picnicking — and for good reason. Bizarre volcanic rock formations, with large holes and caverns, cover the area. Two popular hiking trails run through the volcanic rock.

A Mojave swing demands special talent

Accommodation

There are two family-oriented camp-grounds in the Mojave National Preserve. Backcountry camping is allowed anywhere, so long as you stay half a mile away from the road and a ¼ mile from water sources. There are several designated roadside camping areas as well.

Three information centers service the Mojave National Preserve: the Baker Desert Information Center, the Needles Desert Information Center and the Hole-in-the-

Wall Ranger Station (all of which can be reached by phone at 760-252-6100).

For more information, call 760-255-8800 or log onto the website at www.nps.gov/moja.

Eastern Sierra

This landscape is great for walking or biking in, and the kids will likely want to scramble up boulders, too.

Rock climbing is just one of many activities the Eastern Sierra is known for

The Eastern Sierra is where the desert meets the mountains and where the peaks of the Sierra Nevada range, snow-capped for much of the year, soar regally into the sky above the desert scrub, juniper and ponderosa pine forest. The contrasts are intoxicating and invite even the most dedicated flatlander to linger and gaze upon them.

This varied landscape lends itself to a multitude of cool activities, some of which are unique within the context of the Southwest. Summer offers opportunities to go mountain biking, climbing, hiking, camping and fishing. Winter invites you to go downhill skiing (at world-class Mammoth Mountain, for example), snowshoeing and cross-country skiing, and still take in some fishing as well. The sand dunes and salt flats of nearby Death Valley National Park will inspire you to try a variety of activities year-round.

Just about the only thing you can't do here (compared to other destinations in California) is surf. Few of the places mentioned in this

Biking is another

chapter will be crowded and, outside of weekends and the summer season, you'll likely find you have the Eastern Sierra wilds pretty much to yourselves. That's really nice, when you consider that bustling Los Angeles is just an easy four or five-hour car trip away.

The Eastern Sierra has an incredibly rich history, especially when it comes to Native American culture and the exploits of early gold miners. Around Bishop, however, cattlemen and sheep farmers were the first real settlers. They were convinced that their livestock and families could do no better than live amongst the lush meadows of the Owens River Valley and so they began putting down roots in the early 1800s.

Lone Pine has a similar history, although it was originally established to supply miners with crucial provisions. Ranchers arrived by the mid-1800s and shortly after that the Carson-Colorado Railroad was built through town. Unfortunately, very little

survives from that early era: only a few remnants of adobe walls and the decaying remains of the ghost town Cerro Gordo, located a few miles east of town.

This part of the Eastern Sierra was also once home to the California grizzly bear, which is now sadly extinct. However, it is still home to the California bighorn sheep (an endangered subspecies of Rocky Mountain sheep) and numerous other mammal, reptile, bird and fish populations.

As diverse as the animal wildlife is, it's arguably the plants that are most noteworthy here. The ancient bristlecone pine is by all accounts the oldest surviving tree species in the world. A grove located in the White Mountains (one hour northeast of Bishop) contains several specimens estimated to be at least 4,000 years old.

Other native plant species, while not as celebrated as the bristlecone pine, are remarkable in different ways. The ponderosa pine forests surrounding Mammoth Lakes are easily the most beautiful we've ever seen. Alpine and desert wildflowers are incredibly colorful and varied, too. If you visit Bishop or Lone Pine in the spring, you're almost sure to encounter a visual feast of flowers.

We're sure you'll enjoy your trip to this beautiful area. The following activities and travel suggestions — most of which start from the "bases" of Bishop or Lone Pine — will hopefully allow you to get the most out of your stay.

Bishop
as a
base

Bishop, as a center for adventure travel, is on a par with few other towns

Enjoying an ice cream on Bishop's main street

we've visited. It's a friendly and wholesome place in a spectacular setting, where the landscape strikes a perfect balance between the desert and the mountains. The great granite peaks of the Sierra Nevada Mountains tower overhead and are often capped with snow, while stands of cactus and desert scrub encircle the city.

A few miles north, on the way to Mammoth Lakes, alpine vegetation dominates the landscape and temperatures are noticeably colder (especially when you reach Crowley Summit at 7,500 feet). By comparison, the trip south toward Lone Pine unveils an increasingly dry landscape of high desert, with roadrunners and lizards the animals most likely to be seen.

In addition to the many adventure activities that beckon, Bishop has several star cultural attractions. A number of the restaurants here are excellent; Mexican fare is especially good, as are the offerings of numerous bakeries. Eric Shaatz has been a favorite hangout during our visits, although it tends to cater to tourists. The Mountain Light Gallery showcases photography by the late Galen and Barbara Rowell, and inspires all those who pass through its doors.

There are plenty of good motel options in Bishop, for either a short or a long stay. A number of campgrounds are located in town (or nearby) for those with camping equipment or motorhomes. Check with the local tourist services to get the best advice about available accommodations. The staff (as well as parks service personnel) can also suggest tons of interesting activities. One of the best outings is a visit to the nearby Ancient Bristlecone Pine Forest.

Bristlecone Pine Forest

A visit to the Ancient Bristlecone Pine Forest

is an absolute "must" if you're in the Bishop area during summer or early autumn. For kids and adults alike, it's astonishing to think that some of the trees in this forest were little saplings at the time the great pyramids of Egypt were being constructed. Most of the older trees are believed to be about 4,000 years old, but one that was cut down in nearby Great Basin National Park — known as "Prometheus" — has been estimated to be 4,900 years old.

The Ancient Bristlecone Pine Forest features two main areas containing these fascinating trees: the Schulman Grove and the Patriarch Grove. The former is accessible entirely via paved roads from Bishop. Take Highway 395 south toward Big Pine but turn east onto Highway 168 just north of town. Follow Highway 168 east for 13 miles to reach White Mountain Road. Turn left (north) and drive 10 miles to the Schulman Grove Visitor Center.

The Patriarch Grove is a 12-mile drive north of Schulman Grove on a good-quality dirt road. It features the world's largest bristlecone pine, known as "The Patriarch Tree" on a slope near the tree line.

Bristlecone pine trees can be seen either from the Schulman Grove Visitor Center's parking area or from vantage points along several nature trails that meander through the area. In general, the Ancient Bristlecone Pine Forest is open from mid-May through to the end of October, weather permitting.

Although bristlecone pines are generally believed to be the oldest known living trees, it's interesting to note that some scientists believe the Mojave creosote bush might actually be older.

For information on road closures and travelling conditions in the Ancient Bristlecone Pine Forest, phone 760-873-2500.

Buttermilks

Only 10 miles from Bishop (about 20 minutes by car) is a group of boulders known as the Buttermilk boulders (or just the Buttermilks). They attract lots of local climbers, as well as visitors from throughout the U.S. and Canada. There are many established routes, so you should never feel crowded.

Some of the climbs up the boulders are very difficult, but there are options for every ability level. You can buy a guidebook that lists

Bouldering is awesome in the Buttermilks

them in detail or simply wander around and check out the ones that look most feasible. We recommend carrying a crash pad for the kids (and adults), or spotting kids carefully on the small boulders and perhaps belaying from the tops of the big ones (if you can find a secure stance).

To reach the designated parking area for the Buttermilk boulders when traveling from Bishop, find West Line Road (or Highway 168, right in the town center) and head west for approximately eight miles. Turn right onto Buttermilk Road and continue on the good gravel surface past the first series of Buttermilk boulders to a high point that's home to the Birthday boulders. There should be plenty of parking spots available here, even on a busy day.

If you prefer roped climbing on longer routes, Owen's Gorge might be worth checking out as well. Although it's a little further out of town, it's still close and may be a cooler option if the weather is hot. Drive about 14 miles north of Bishop on Highway 395 and then turn right onto Gorge Road. From this point, it's about three miles to the south parking area, four and a half miles to the central parking area and six miles to the north parking area.

There are almost 500 routes in the Owen's Gorge area, ranging in difficulty from 5.7 to 5.13 (on the America standard scale) and with most of them geared toward sport climbers. A few traditional lines exist, too.

World-class fishing

Bishop is justifiably famous for its trout fishing. If your family enjoys fishing, then this place is tough to beat. Very large fish are caught regularly in the Eastern Sierra region and hooking enough pan-sized trout for supper is generally an easy task — at least during the year's peak fishing seasons. The Department of Fish and Game and Bishop's Adopt-a-Creek program help ensure that local creeks and lakes are protected and kept well-stocked.

Mono Lake's lunar landscapes lie just beyond Mammoth Lakes

Bishop

Travel times to:

Lone Pine: via Highway 395 (south); 1 hour and 15 minutes
Los Angeles: via Highway 10 (east), Highway 15 (north), Highway 395 (north); 5 hours and 15 minutes
Reno: via Highway 395 (north); 4 hours
Mammoth Mountain: via Highway 395 (north); 1 hour

a brief stop here is highly recommended, especially if no one in your family has ever had a close-up look at a lava flow.

Red cinder cones and dark basaltic lava flows dominate the views in all directions. As testaments to the great forces of volcanism, they offer children a natural history lesson that's not soon forgotten.

If you're planning a summer visit, try fishing at some of the lakes and streams in the high country. The trout here are notoriously hungry for almost any type of bait. During late autumn, winter and early spring, Bishop Creek is an excellent choice for casting a line, although you should check with local authorities regarding seasonal closures. The Owens River and Pleasant Valley Reservoir are almost always good spots, too.

World-class skiing

In terms of great skiing, the Mammoth Mountain ski area certainly lives up to its name. Sprawled across nearly 4,000 acres of varied terrain, it is one of America's biggest ski areas and is known for its fresh powder conditions. Nearly 30 lifts climb to the top of a dozen bowls and some of them routinely stay open right through June!

For more information on the Mammoth Mountain ski area, phone 800-MAMMOTH, or 760-934-0745.

Big Pine lava flows

South of Big Pine (on the road that runs from Bishop to Lone Pine) are the Big Pine volcanic fields of Crater Mountain. Even

Lone Pine

as a base

For a town of less than 2,000 people, Lone Pine is blessed with remarkable diversity. Geographically, it's bordered on one side by the highest point in the lower 48 states (Mount Whitney, at 14,490 feet) and on the other side by the lowest point (Badwater in Death Valley, at 282 feet below sea level). That means that your family can play in snow and desert sand in the same afternoon.

Historically, the town has been home to everyone from gold miners and silver miners seeking their fortune during the 1800s to the people who built the Los Angeles Aqueduct in the 1920s. During the Second World War, Japanese-Americans were held in detainment camps located nearby. Over the years, Hollywood crews have shot more than 250 films in the area.

Today, Lone Pine is mainly populated by outdoor enthusiasts and artisans. Their influence is evident in annual events like the Wild West Marathon (one of the toughest runs in North America) and the Lone

How Lone Pine got its name

Airborne over Lone Pine

The town of Lone Pine is named after a solitary pine tree that was found at the mouth of Lone Pine Canyon when the town was founded in the 1860s. It was established to provide supplies to the gold mining and silver mining communities of Kearsarg, Cerro Gordo and Darwin — and to farmers and ranchers who settled here later on. That old pine tree has long since vanished, after being destroyed in a flood.

Pine Film Festival (an event that sees many locals and visitors dress up in colorful Wild West garb).

Despite its relatively small size, Lone Pine bustles with activity year-round and boasts many amenities for travelers. There are about a dozen motels, inns and bed-and-breakfast accommodations to choose from in Lone Pine, with another half-dozen available 15 miles to the north in the town of Independence. Local restaurants and grocery stores offer a wide range of choices at decent prices.

Most of your time here will no doubt be spent trying out some of the activities and itineraries listed below.

Manzanar Detainment Camp

Despite being a fairly bleak place to bring the family, Manzanar can teach your kids some valuable history. This camp housed more than 10,000 Japanese-Americans during the Second World War. The detainees were not criminals, but were Americans who just happened to have Japanese ancestry.

The camp was closed in 1954 and is quite dilapidated now. To get there, take Highway 395 until you're about 10 miles from Lone Pine. You'll know when you've arrived when you spot two monuments at the camp entrance on the west side of the highway.

Local fishing spots

The streams and ponds around Lone Pine are filled with rainbow, golden and brown trout, as well as catfish and bass. It's possible to fish year-round at Diaz Lake (just south of Lone Pine) and along the Owens River. Permits are required in some areas.

For more information, call 760-876-4444.

One of Lone Pine's more colorful residents

Locomotive No. 18

This old, narrow-gauge locomotive hauled both freight and folks up and down the Owens Valley for years. It was put to rest some decades ago and its aging — but timelessly romantic — hulk now stands in Dehy Park in the town of Independence. It's a nice spot for a picnic, with lots of shady trees and a touch of Old West flair.

Eastern California Museum

This small but likable museum describes the natural and cultural history of the region. You'll learn about Native American and pioneer heritage, the Manzanar Detainment Camp and more. It also has an excellent collection of books on subjects of local interest. The museum is open every day except Tuesday, from 10 a.m. to 4 p.m.

For more information, call 619-878-0364.

Biking is a great way to get around in the Alabama Hills

Alabama Hills

Take one glance at the Alabama Hills above Lone Pine and you're sure to be taken back to some memorable scenes from the movies of yesteryear. Hollywood has filmed over 250 movies in the region (including the first Lone Ranger) and crews still return from time to time to shoot scenes in the very atmospheric Alabama Hills.

This landscape is great for walking or biking in, and the kids will likely want to scramble up boulders, too. That's fine, but just observe the usual safety precautions. With the rugged spine of the Sierra Nevada Mountains forming a stunning backdrop in the distance, it's a great place to take photographs of the family, too.

Lone Pine

Travel times to:

Death Valley: via Highway 395 (south), Highway 136 (east), Highway 190 (east); 2 hours and 45 minutes

Bishop: via Highway 395 (north); 1 hour and 15 minutes

Los Angeles: via Highway 10 (east), Highway 15 (north), Highway 395 (north); 4 hours

Las Vegas: via Highway 395 (south), Highway 136/190 (east), Highway 374 (east), Highway 95 (south); 5 hours and 15 minutes

Mount Whitney: via Whitney Portal Road; 30 minutes

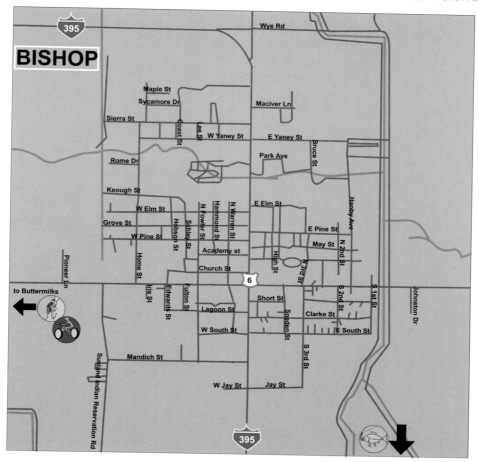

BISHOP

Lone Pine is on the doorstep of a huge expanse of rugged desert terrain

Death Valley National Park

Despite its ominous name, Death Valley is actually home to all sorts of wildlife and about 900 plant species inhabit the area.

as a base Death Valley National Park is one of America's newest national parks, having been upgraded from "national monument" status less than 20 years ago. At almost 3.5 million acres, it's also one of the country's biggest. It showcases a broad range of topography and a variety of flora and fauna. Kit foxes and rattlesnakes are common sights, but in some places you'll see nothing at all — not even a speck of vegetation.

Death Valley has long been a favorite location for Hollywood filmmakers. At least 100 movies and television shows have been shot here since the mid-1920s, including Star Wars (1977), Tarzan (1951) and The Doors (1991). Its dramatic landscapes are "picture perfect" and often appear otherworldly (a great attribute for filming a science fiction movie).

Death Valley landscapes.

Death Valley landscapes.

The park's beauty is subtle. Watching the sun set over sand dunes at Stovepipe Wells is an unforgettable experience, as is seeing the morning light creep across salt polygons in The Devil's Playground. If your visit coincides with the blossoming of spring flowers (March or April), this magical place can offer a visual feast of colour and beauty.

Perhaps Death Valley's greatest claim to fame is that it's home to the Western Hemisphere's lowest land elevation: 282 feet below sea level, at Badwater. It's also the driest place in North America, recording an average of less than two inches of rainfall per year.

But Death Valley National Park also contains some high mountain country. The Panamint Mountain Range, which towers over Death Valley's western flank, is commonly capped with snow during the winter months.

The low elevation of the valley floor makes it a delightful place to visit during the cooler months of the year, with average temperatures 20º higher than nearby Lone Pine. During the summer, however, it can be an uncomfortably hot travel destination. Midday temperatures in July and August exceed 100º F on most days.

Try to travel here during the cooler months, especially if your family enjoys outdoor activities. Even if you arrive during the late spring or early fall, it's a good idea to get up early or set out late in the day. (See the section on sand dune exploration below.) This way, your kids will be spared the worst of Death Valley's blistering heat. Regardless of when you visit, remember to always travel with lots of water!

Death Valley has nine campgrounds, two of which take reservations: Furnace Creek and Texas Spring (call 1-800-365-2267). The rest operate on a "first come, first served" basis. There are also about three million acres of open space where you can find

World's Toughest Footrace

When you consider that the Lone Pine area is home to some of the world's most extreme terrain, it's not surprising that it's also home to the world's most extreme footrace: the Badwater Ultramarathon.

The 135-mile course runs from the lowest point in the contiguous United States (Badwater Basin, at 282 feet below sea level) to a very high one (Whitney Portal, at 8,360 feet). That's challenging enough, but what makes this race "ultra bad" is that it's run in the middle of the summer when temperatures often climb to over 130° F.

Each July, 70 to 80 competitors lace up their running shoes and stock up on water in a gruelling effort that's not so much about finishing first as it is about just finishing — period. Typically, up to half of the contestants drop out due to dehydration or heat exhaustion, even though they're usually elite athletes. (So far, there have been no fatalities on the course.)

The first person to complete the race, after failing in three previous attempts, was Al Arnold in 1977. Since celebrating that achievement, however, he's reportedly never returned. It must have been the water.

free backcountry camping spots, but check with park service personnel before pitching your tent.

If camping out doesn't appeal to you — or if it's just too hot, windy or cold — lodging is available within the park at Furnace Creek Ranch, the Furnace Creek Inn and the Stovepipe Wells Village. The latter has a swimming pool that's open to the general public for a nominal fee, which makes for an awesome plunge on a hot day. (Phone 760-786-2387 for details.)

For more information, call 760-786-3200 or check out the website at www.nps.gov/deva.

Death Valley Junior Ranger program

Despite its ominous name, Death Valley is actually home to all sorts of wildlife and about 900 plant species inhabit the area. Since this is one of the hottest and driest places in North America, the flora and fauna have had to find ways to adapt to the extreme conditions. Most of the animals in Death Valley are nocturnal and therefore avoid the worst of the heat. Plants have root systems that either fan out beneath the ground or have roots that plunge deep down to collect water from below the surface.

Kids will learn about these adaptive techniques — and much more science besides — if they participate in Death Valley's Junior Ranger Program. It's more comprehensive than similar programs offered in some other national parks, and workbooks for children of all ages are available at the visitor center.

The booklet has 15 projects for kids to work on. It's suggested that children aged six and under should finish four of them, those aged 7-10 should complete six projects and children older than 11 should do at least nine. The reward is the coveted Death Valley Junior Ranger badge, a near-replica of the National Park Service badge.

Death Valley's sand dunes are great fun by day

and in the evening

Climbing Sand Dunes

Death Valley has some of the most photographed sand dunes in the world. They're big, too, with the largest one rising almost 150 feet from the bottom to the very top. They're also very accessible, just a short hike off the road near Stovepipe Wells or up a short gravel road on the southeast side.

We recommend taking the first route if you plan to climb any of the higher dunes. Drive southeast from Stovepipe Wells (toward Furnace Creek) and park in the large gravel area on the left (east) side of the road. Simply aim for the largest dune you can see and maintain a steady course, as you rise over each crest of sand and slide down into the little valleys in between.

Once you get past the initial thorny vegetation and reach the sand, there's little danger to watch out for. Kids can kick off their shoes and socks and run to their heart's content, or they can roll down the dune. What could be more fun?

If it's really hot during your visit to Death Valley, consider exploring the dunes in the evening. All you'll need is a headlamp for each person in the group, along with plenty of water and a few snacks. Watch for kit foxes in the small, vegetated troughs you'll come across. We had one scamper by within a few feet of us while we sat outside one evening after sunset.

Golden Canyon

This canyon has particularly beautiful coloration and the short (one mile) access route makes it an easy outing for kids. At the highest point of land, you'll be treated to a great view of the central portion of Death Valley. If the visibility is good, you'll be able to spot the sand dunes, Stovepipe Wells and other places.

Start out from the Golden Canyon parking area, two miles south of the junction of Highway 190 with Highway 267. The trail is easy to find and follow. Look for the Red Cathedral - a natural formation - about half a mile up the canyon, beyond the last numbered trail marker.

As with any outing in Death Valley, make sure you bring along lots of water and a few snacks. Wearing decent footwear is also a good idea, but hiking boots are probably not necessary.

Scotty's Castle

Scotty's Castle, also called Death Valley

This is the aptly named Golden Canyon, in Death Valley

Ranch, is one of the most curious human creations in the Southwest. Built as a vacation home by "Death Valley Scotty" at a cost of around $2 million, it's now a National Park Service treasure and is open to the general public.

The "castle" is nestled in a relatively lush canyon northeast of Stovepipe Wells within a beautiful oasis, but it's the interior environment that's most stunning. Here you'll witness amazing technological innovations and incredible craftsmanship, given the 1930's era in which it was built.

Somewhat mysterious, a little whimsical and utterly unique, Scotty's Castle is well worth a visit. To get there, drive to the junction of Highway 190 with Highway 267 (about five miles east of Stovepipe Wells) and then drive north another 40 miles.

Geometric patterns of salt can be found near Badwater

Scotty's Castle is open every day from 8:30 a.m. to 5 p.m., with tours of the main house beginning at 9 a.m. and conducted on a "first come, first served" basis.

For more information, phone 760-786-2392.

Badwater Salt Flat

This is a great little hike (half a mile to the edge and five miles across), if for no other reason than being able to say that you've walked across the lowest point of land in the Western Hemisphere. It's absolutely level, but walking even half its length will still be a scorching experience, so think twice about doing it during the height of summer. If you visit just after a rainstorm, the Badwater Salt Flat might take on the appearance of a shallow lake, if only temporarily.

Start the hike from the Badwater parking area, 17 miles south of Highway 190 on Badwater Road. There's not much of a trail to follow, but the way forward should be pretty obvious. Remember to take lots of water!

Zion National Park

Zion retains an impressive array of wildlife. There are 14 different types of lizards, desert bighorn sheep, mule deer, porcupines and mountain lions.

Zion National Park is often the first (and sometimes the only) great canyonland park that people visit when they some to the Southwest, primarily because of its close proximity to Las Vegas and its accessibility from Interstate 15. They could hardly do any better. Zion is one of America's finest national parks, with fantastic canyons, picturesque glades, great amenities and much more.

A free shuttle bus travels from town to all the major points of interest in Zion National Park. This shuttle was introduced in the 1970s to counteract the environmental damage resulting from millions of visitors driving their own vehicles along the park's narrow, winding road.

The first stop inside the park is at the Zion

Taking in the view over Zion's southwest entry point

Zion's main camping area hugs the picturesque Virgin River

Canyon Visitor Center. The staff can provide you with all the information you need to hike nearby and on the backcountry trails in the park. There's also an excellent bookstore at the center, with several guidebooks that cover the area in detail. (Some of them are geared specifically toward family adventuring.) Nearby, the Zion Adventure Company is a great resource for outdoor equipment rentals.

For such a heavily visited park, Zion retains an impressive array of wildlife. There are 14 different types of lizards, desert bighorn sheep, mule deer, porcupines, mountain lions and many other types of creatures. Kids will be impressed to learn that a mountain lion can leap 30 feet from a standing start.

For centuries, animals shared the terrain with the Puebloan and Paiute native people. It wasn't until the late 1700s that the first non-natives arrived. In 1776, members of the Dominguez/Escalante expedition traveled to the area while looking for an overland route from Santa Fe to California. In the late 1800s, Mormon settlers established several towns near the park, including Springdale, Hurricane and St. George.

Zion National Park has been attracting tourists since the road through the park was completed in the 1930s. The two-lane, red rock thoroughfare that winds through the steep canyons was built during the Great Depression. It was a "make work" project that involved thousands of laborers, who were paid the bare minimum to get the job done. It's doubtful that building the road today (given the high cost of labor) would be financially viable. This road now provides visitors with easy access to the park and is easy to negotiate, even for RVs.

Along with the community of Springfield (which is located just outside the park's western boundary), Zion National Park is one of the Southwest's finest adventure destinations. Hiking is particularly good here and the facilities are well-developed. Mountain biking, horseback riding, rock climbing and "canyoneering" are all very popular here and in nearby areas.

Zion's Junior Ranger program encourages the exploration of its wide-open spaces, as well as narrow ones

In short, Zion National Park is a place where you can hang out with the kids quite comfortably for several days. If you don't have time to venture much further into the wilderness, it will at least give you a taste for the magnificence of the Southwest.

Below are a few itineraries and activities that will help your family discover the region's natural beauty.

Zion Junior Ranger Explorer Program

In addition to providing a self-guided Junior Ranger program (like most other national parks), Zion has a fully guided program. Intended for kids between the ages of six and 12, the Junior Ranger Explorer program will introduce children to the park through hands-on activities, hikes and nature lessons.

The emphasis is on local animals, geology and archeology. Kids will receive pins and certificates for completing the session. The program runs from May until August, with one morning and one afternoon session. The cost of the program is $2 per child. To sign up, go to the Zion Nature Center, which is half a mile north of the park entrance. (Note that the park shuttle bus doesn't stop at this facility.)

For more information, call 435-772-0169.

Zion Park Shuttle

This bus stops at all of the major facilities in the park. The drive alone, as the road winds its way up through towering red rock, is worth the trip. You'll pass pinnacles that look like organ pipes, others that resemble jagged teeth and still others that replicate majestic castles. Most of the route runs parallel to the Virgin River.

Going on a few hikes and paying a visit to the Zion Human History Museum (where a 22-minute orientation film plays throughout the day) will only add to the experience.

Another nice thing about the bus is that it's free. Try to catch it as early in the morning as possible during the high season - late spring, summer, early autumn - to avoid crowds. The driver will provide informative commentary along the way and probably point out a rock climber or two, perched up high on one of the nearby rock faces.

For more information, call 1-888-518-7070.

Itineraries

1 Riverside Walk

Distance: 2 miles (or longer, if the canyon walk is included)
Time: 1½ hours
Difficulty: Easy to Moderate

The paved part of this hike is nice, but it's the narrow canyon and stream beyond that the kids will enjoy most. This is an excellent route to hike on a hot day since it's mostly shaded — thanks to the steep canyon wall on either side.

To get to the trailhead, take the free Zion National Park shuttle bus to the final stop at "Temple of Sinawava". As you begin walking, you'll probably be joined by a throng of other people. Since this is a relatively short and flat walk, people young and old seem willing to give it a try. For this reason, try to avoid weekends, get there early and definitely (if the water levels permit) walk upstream past the one mile mark.

As you stroll along the paved path (which is coated with pink dust from the nearby rocks), you'll slowly make your way upstream past some surprisingly lush vegetation. Thanks to an occasional intense rain shower and the spring runoff, this area has turned into a "desert swamp" of sorts. Fern and moss pro-

Keeping cool on the upstream walk

Mormons in the Land of Zion

When hiking in Zion National Park, it doesn't take long for a visitor to recognize its Mormon roots. Trails that pass landmarks like the "Great White Throne" and the "Altar of Sacrifice" make sure of that.

But who are the Mormons and how did they wind up here?

The Mormon faith was founded in 1830 by Joseph Smith, in Fayette, New York. Today, there are more than 12 million adherents worldwide. Most of them live outside North America, thanks to the religion's very active volunteer missionary program.

As well as believing in modern prophets, Mormons have — until fairly recently — practiced polygamy. They also adhere to a strict dietary code that excludes alcohol and caffeine. The use of tobacco is also prohibited, so it's ironic that tobacco played a big role in the early development of the area.

Mormons were first sent here from Salt Lake City in the 1850s and 1860s to grow cotton, which was no longer available from back east because of the Civil War. Some of those people established settlements near Springdale and used them as bases to explore the canyon.

By 1861, Isaac Behunin began growing tobacco on the canyon floor, along with fruit and vegetables. Farming, along with the grazing of livestock on nearby plateaus, continued until 1909. That's when the area was turned into a national monument — and then 10 years later into a national park.

vide ground cover and cottonwood trees stretch up from the canyon floor.

The only real risks associated with continuing beyond the end of the paved path are flash floods or falling debris, when the upper reaches of the canyon freeze during the winter. Stop in at the Zion Canyon Visitor Center to check the current conditions. If you get the "all clear", find a walking stick, wear a pair of shoes you don't mind getting wet and press on. You'll be rewarded with a cool stream to wade in (a welcome reprieve from the desert heat in summer), stunning waterfalls cascading down cliffs and intriguingly textured canyon walls.

Exploring some of the narrower bends in the canyon is particularly exciting for kids, since they'll feel like they're very much in their own world. It's generally safe for them to do so, since there are few places where the water will rise past their knees or the current is strong.

2 Canyon Overlook Walk

Distance: 1 mile (round trip)
Time: ¾ to 1½ hours
Difficulty: Easy

The Canyon Overlook walk is a quick and easy way to get a glimpse of the canyon. You'll also get a good look at the road as it snakes its way up and disappears into the long tunnel system you've just come through (if you approached from the west). The trail is quite pretty and there's little change in elevation.

The only downside to this route is that it's very likely that other people will be walking along it at the same time, thanks to it being so close to the highway. To avoid crowds, try to arrive early in the morning or late in the day.

When you arrive, park in one of the pull-outs located on the east side of the mile-long tunnel. Walk down to the tunnel and

The Canyon Overlook offers spectacular views

look for the park warden's kiosk. The trail-head is just behind it. Make sure you pick up a trail guide here, since it describes the flora, fauna and geology of the area, among other things.

Although this walk is short, it's quite diverse in terms of its scenery and terrain. Start off by walking up a natural sandstone staircase. The route then follows a narrow pathway strewn with pink sand and meanders over large, flat rock slabs.

Soon you'll cross over a cliff-hugging wooden walkway (equipped with handrails) and walk underneath massive stone overhangs. Keep an eye on younger kids, since there are some steep drop-offs along the way.

There are also railings at the lookout, which you'll appreciate when you see how sheer the cliffs are. As you look down over the winding road that passes through Zion, ask the kids if they can also spot the network of game trails. (They're a little harder to see.)

3 : Emerald Pools

Distance: 0.6 miles to the lower pool or 1.5 miles to the upper pool
Time: 1-2 hours (return)
Difficulty: Easy

This is one of the easiest and most scenic trails in Zion National Park. The trick is to arrive at the starting point early in the morning, before the arrival of the crowds and the intense heat of the desert sun. To get to the trailhead, first take the shuttle bus to Zion Lodge.

Directional signs will lead you across a small bridge and to the start of two routes. Take the one that follows the river. It will eventually pass behind cascading waterfalls — a very cool experience. After less than half an hour of gentle climbing, you'll arrive at the first set of pools.

If the trail here is crowded with people and

your kids still have lots of energy, you may want to continue on to the upper pools. Fewer people visit them, but an even more impressive waterfall awaits you (in the fall and spring, anyway).

4 Angels Landing

Distance: 5 miles (each way)
Time: 5-7 hours (return)
Difficulty: Difficult (there's a narrow ridge crest and a 1,490-foot elevation gain)

Angel's landing is one of the most exciting hikes we've ever completed as a family in the Southwest, with a view that's simply second to none. Neither you nor your kids will forget this trek. It's not for the faint of heart, though, particularly during the traverse along its uppermost section. Here, hikers must scramble along a narrow, rocky crest perched

The final approach to Angels' Landing is straight ahead

above an absolutely vertical drop of several thousand feet to the valley below. It's not a particularly good route for a hot day, owing to the considerable elevation gain over several sun-baked slopes.

Take lots of water and snacks with you. A rope and harness for the final section is not a bad idea either. Be prepared to watch your kids very carefully and hold their hands on the final exposed section.

The trailhead is located right across from The Grotto picnic area, which can be reached easily by using the shuttle bus.

You'll climb gradually at first and then more steeply through an interesting mix of desert vegetation and rocks, but always on a very good path.

The final approach to Angel's Landing is safeguarded by a chain link handrail at first. Advise your kids to hold onto this carefully as they scramble up to an exposed ridge section. From this point on, we advise that you hold their hands until everyone is safely seated on the Landing crest. Do the same thing on the way down, since it's more likely that a slip will occur while going down than heading up.

The final approach to Angel's Landing is safeguarded by a chain link handrail

cuisine.

Springdale

as a base Springdale is a great base for exploring Zion National Park. Situated on the doorstep of the park's west entrance, it provides all the basic amenities needed for your family to stay in the area for a few days.

There are about a dozen motels, hotels and inns to choose from. There's also an RV park here, although all three campgrounds inside the park (located within 2 km) allow RVs and are about half the price. They don't have hook-ups and shower facilities, however. The town has a couple of grocery stores that offer more variety than the store that's inside the park, which stocks everything you'll need to outfit yourself for day hikes. Restaurant offerings range from Chinese food to pizza joints and Southwest

Activities in the Zion area:

Zion Canyon Giant Screen Theater

This six-storey-high edifice at the entrance to Zion National Park is one of the world's largest movie screens. To get there, take Springdale's shuttle bus and ask the driver to drop you off at the theater. The main feature is Treasure of the Gods, which explores some of the park's hidden areas and the legends that surround them. Between April and October, there are shows every hour on the hour. In the off-season, Hollywood films often play here, albeit on a screen that's nine times larger than the one at your local theater.

For more information, call 435-772-2400.

Rock Climbing and "Canyoneering"

The Zion Adventure Company, located in Springdale, offers a variety of courses for novice and experienced climbers. There are also courses for kids aged five and up. Equipment is available for rent if you pre-fer to do some self-guided exploring. The Zion Adventure Company is located on the corner of Lion Boulevard and Highway 9, across from the Quality Inn.

For more information, call 435-772-1001.

Springdale
Travel times to:

St. George: via Highway 9 (west); 45 minutes
Las Vegas: via Highway 9 (west), Highway 15 (south); 2 hours and 45 minutes
Zion National Park: via Highway 9 (west); 5 minutes
Kanab: via Highway 9 (west), Highway 89 (south); 1 hour

Zion's eastern landscapes are more typical of other parts of southern Utah

American Southwest

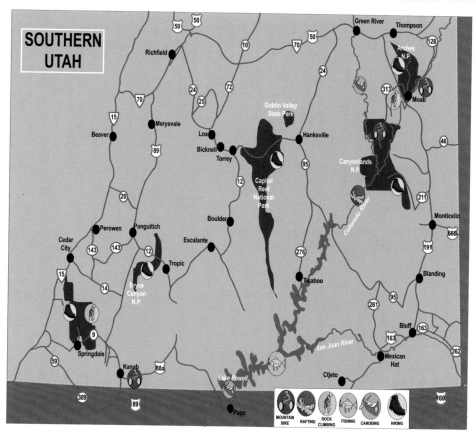

SOUTHERN UTAH

Bryce Canyon National Park To Capital Reef National Park

Erosion caused by freezing, thawing, wind and rain has done much to sculpt the soft limestone rock into formations called hoodoos.

as a
base

You've likely seen pictures of Bryce Canyon National Park even if you've never visited it before. Rows of slender, crumbling sandstone pillars — sometimes snow-capped — create a fairyland of geological wonders, with light patterns and colors that photographers just can't resist.

Bryce's intriguing rock formations

The park was named after the Mormon pioneer Ebenezer Bryce and was established as a national park in 1924. Not surprisingly, one of the best places to see Bryce Canyon in all its glory (especially at sunrise) is a spot called Fairyland Point. An amphitheatre full of strange rock formations draws in the viewer and the scene then stretches out toward distant mesas and high desert forests many miles away. Bryce Canyon boasts some of the best visibility conditions anywhere in the world. On a good day, it's possible to see objects that are 200 miles away.

So how did the characteristic Bryce Canyon topography develop? Erosion caused by freezing, thawing, wind and rain has done much to sculpt the soft limestone rock into formations called hoodoos. It's also created bizarre window and fin shapes, and has been responsible for the development of the region's characteristic slot canyons.

The unique landscape (with its

beautifully coloured rocks, delightful Ponderosa pine and juniper forests, and a diverse resident wild-life population) makes Bryce Canyon a great place to visit — even if you can only stay for a short time. Numerous interesting hiking pos-sibilities will tempt your family to stay longer. It should be noted that almost all of the routes descend from a high elevation to a low one, meaning that you and the kids will have to hike back uphill to return to the car.

Trail views along the Fairyland Loop

A couple of worthwhile biking trips near the edge of the park might warrant a longer stay, if you have the time available. We provide a few pointers for those routes below.

Activities in the area:

Because of Bryce Canyon's high elevation (the visitor center is located at 7,894 feet), off-season travel is somewhat limited here. It can get quite cold up top, even in April or October! Be prepared for chilly tempera-tures unless you visit in late spring, summer or early fall.

1 Fairyland Loop

Distance: 8 miles (in total)
Time: 3-4 hours
Difficulty: Moderate

This is as pretty a hike as any other in the park and the first one you'll come across after passing through the park gates. Even if you choose not to descend all the way to Tower Bridge, the first part of the trail is quite rewarding. (It's a fair way down, how-ever, which could mean a laborious hike back up — especially if the weather is hot.)

Just after you enter the park, look for a sign

on the left directing you to Fairyland Point. In a little over a mile, you'll reach the parking area and the trailhead. The path first traverses a steep hillside and then descends to Fairyland Canyon, before climbing again prior to the final descent into Campbell Canyon.

The trail crosses Tower Bridge (it's unlikely that you'll see any water underneath it) and begins a 1.5-mile climb up to the Rim Trail near Sunrise Point. Although it's slightly out of the way, it's worth hiking the short distance to Sunrise Point to take in the spectacular vista. When you're ready to leave, retrace your steps along the Rim Trail and follow the road north for 2.5 miles to reach the parking area.

2 Biking near Ruby's

Distance: **8 miles (in total)**
Time: **3-4 hours**
Difficulty: **Moderate**

If you've brought mountain bikes along, you can check out some fun biking terrain just on the outskirts of the park, near Ruby's Lodge and Campground. Off-road biking is not allowed within Bryce Canyon National Park, so staying outside the park boundaries is mandatory.

A fairly short loop is described here, but longer variations are possible. Start on the horse trail right across the road from Ruby's. Follow this southeast for about 1.5 miles to the eastern rim's edge. Here, exquisite panorama of hoodoos and distant mesas await you.

This trail connects with a number of Nordic skiing, bike and horse trails that head north along the rim edge. Staying just outside of the national park boundary, these relatively flat and easy-to-follow paths all eventually lead back to the pavement. Follow whichever one grabs your fancy or whichever one is the least muddy (especially in spring).

Biking is allowed only outside the park's boundaries

Kanab

as a
base

"Location, location, location." How better could you describe the attributes of this interesting little town?

Surrounded by no fewer than four national parks, Kanab is a perfect base for outdoor adventure. Within a two-hour drive, you could be tumbling off the top of the Coral Pink Sand Dunes, climbing the red rocks of Zion National Park or rafting down the blue water of the Colorado River.

But the town itself is appealing, too. Nicknamed Utah's "Little Hollywood" for all the movies that have been filmed here, Kanab has five movie sets located in the immediate vicinity. It's not difficult to understand why, once you stop to look around. The Vermilion Cliffs tower over the town to the west and the east, reflecting the rich red and orange hues of the desert (especially at sunrise and sunset). Dramatic canyons, cut into the rock by ancient streams, border the local roads.

Best Friends Animal Shelter

With close to 2,000 abused or abandoned pets on-site, this is the largest "no-kill" animal shelter in the world. You'll find horses, burros, dogs, cats, rabbits and birds among those being cared for.

Hundreds of volunteers, many traveling here from across the country, donate their time to the shelter and the upkeep of its animals. A tour of the facility is offered daily. To get there, drive five miles north of Kanab on Highway 89 and turn off at the Kanab Canyon exit. For more information, call 435-644-2001.

The classic and historic Parry Lodge

All of this beauty came at a cost to Kanab's original settlers, however. Mormon pioneers unsuccessfully tried to irrigate the area in the 1860s, resulting in massive flooding in 1883. Ranching supplanted farming as the industry of choice from that point forward.

Film crews provided a boost to the economy as early as the 1920s. Since then, nearly 200 movies have been shot in the area. Tourism has also done its share for this community of 5,000 people. There's a wide selection of motels and restaurants along Highway 89 that have catered for decades to people traveling to the nearby national parks of Bryce Canyon, Zion and the Grand Canyon.

Today, more and more families are using Kanab as their "home base" to explore the region. The following attractions help explain why.

Parry Lodge

We don't make a habit of endorsing any specific accommodations in this guidebook series, but the Parry Lodge is different. It's a piece of living history that you can enjoy during an overnight stay and we highly recommend doing so.

Inside the lodge, you'll see hundreds of signed portraits of movie stars who've stayed in Kanab since the 1930s, including John Wayne, Roy Rogers, Don Knotts, Tim Conway, George Hamilton, Fess Parker and Patricia Blair. Their legacy lives on in a tranquil, yesteryear ambience.

Off-season - late autumn to early spring - rates make staying at the motel at those times particularly tempting. We're certain you won't regret it.

For more information, call 1-888-289-1722.

Frontier Movie Town

How would you like to be transported right back to the Wild West? There are no fewer than five movie sets in the vicinity of Kanab and the most impressive is Frontier Movie Town. It served as a set for The Outlaw Josie Wells (starring Clint Eastwood), Desperate Hours (Anthony Hopkins) and One Little Indian (James Garner) — among others.

You can watch reenactments of gunfights at sundown or dress in western garb and join in the action. The fully maintained Old West town is located right in the middle of Kanab at 297 West Center Street. There's a gift shop there, as well as a saloon and cook shack dishing out cowboy cuisine. Dinner shows feature the guests as movie stars.

For more information, call 435-644-5337.

Moqui Cave

The largest collection of dinosaur tracks in southern Utah, a fluorescent mineral display and an impressive collection of Native American artifacts are just a few reasons to check out Moqui Cave. It's a fun (if slightly kitschy) tourist stop that's been around since the 1950s. It offers a shady reprieve from the summer sun and is located just off the road you'll take to get to the Coral Pink Sand Dunes. To reach the Moqui Cave, head five miles north of Kanab on Highway 89.

For more information, call 435-644-2987.

Squaw Trail

Squaw Trail is an easy-to-moderate walk that will provide your family with spectacular views of the Kanab area. There are two lookouts along the way. The first is one mile along the trail (with a 400-foot gain in elevation) and the second is 1½ miles along (with an 800-foot gain in elevation).

If you take your time, kids can handle the trail quite easily, since the steeper sections are broken up by long, flat stretches. Keep an eye out for jack-rabbits along the way.

The views from the top are stunning in every direction. To the north are the pink cliffs of the Grand Staircase and Bryce Canyon, to the south is Arizona and the massive Kaibab Plateau, to the west are the pinnacles and buttes of Zion National Park, and to the east is the forested Wygaret Plateau.

Pack a lunch to take with you and don't forget to bring water. To get to the trailhead, make your way to the end of 100 East Street and look for the path just past the city park.

Horseback Riding

Several companies in the Kanab area offer horseback riding packages, ranging in duration from one hour to one week. Many of the routes retrace the paths taken by famous outlaws like Butch Cassidy and Jesse James. With Bryce Canyon National Park and Zion National Park both less than 1½ hours away by car, there are literally hundreds of trails nearby.

Allen's Trail Rides (435-644-8150) and Scenic Rim Trail Rides (800-679-5859) offer short and long rides and both cater to families.

Coral Pink Sand Dunes

Just a short drive from Kanab (on the way to Zion National Park) is the turnoff to the Coral Pink Sand Dunes. These are a series of small but beautifully colored dunes that are easily accessible, just 12 miles from the turnoff.

If you're not planning a trip to the larger dunes of Death Valley or elsewhere, the Coral Pink Sand Dunes are worth a quick trip. The only downside is that access to the dunes must be shared with off-road vehicles, which can be loud and intimidating at times. During both of our trips into the dunes, however, the drivers have been courteous and careful when they've spotted us hiking along.

Entering the park and becoming one with it

Admittedly, the sight of dune buggies racing across the sand (particularly from the crest of the highest dune), can be entertaining — especially for kids who've never seen them in action before. The vehicles can't make it up the steeper slopes though, so it's absolutely safe for your kids to run up, jump on or fall down those.

There's also a great little campground at this state park, with the sites well-spaced between stands of juniper trees. Both RV and tent camping is permitted. The walking trail that heads into the dunes begins right at the campground and is separate from the vehicle access point. Watch for passing vehicles at the crossing point just past the observation area.

East Of Bryce

Kodachrome Basin State Park

Hoodoos become spires and spires become pinnacles in a park that's full of red rock chimneys. The whole scene becomes downright Christmas-like when snow covers the area, but it's incredibly colorful at any other time.

A National Geographic Society expedition that visited the area back in 1949 must have found it all very photogenic. They were the people who named the park.

There are several hiking and biking routes in Kodachrome Basin State Park that are suitable for families. Horseback and stagecoach rides are also available. A good campsite in the park has all the amenities necessary for an evening or two of camping out.

Kodachrome Basin State Park is located nine miles southeast of Cannonville, off Highway 12. Watch for the directional signs while driving east from Bryce Canyon.

For more information, call 435-679-8562 or log onto www.stateparks.utah.gov.

Exploring a slot canyon in Grand Staircase-Escalante

Grand Staircase-Escalante National Monument

Although not as well-known as other natural attractions in the vicinity, this is a place of stunning red rock arches, slot canyons and waterfalls. The twisted juniper trees that line Highway 12 look like they've just popped out of a Dr. Seuss book.

The area is a hiker's paradise. One route that's suitable for families runs to Lower Calf Creek Falls. It's a four-hour jaunt (return) that will take you through classic canyon scenery on its way to the falls, which are 126 feet tall. There's also a little beach and wading area at the foot of the falls.

To get to the trailhead, go east on Highway 12 (past the settlement of Escalante) toward

An outside and inside view of Capital Reef's exquisite little schoolhouse

Torrey

On the western outskirts of Capital Reef National Park is the picturesque and artistic hamlet of Torrey. With a population of only 120 people, it manages to support a gallery, bookstore and a great little café. It also has a gas station and market to stock up on essential supplies. You'd be hard pressed to find a better road stop anywhere, especially in the middle of a hot day.

Capitol Reef National Park

This is where Butch Cassidy and the Wild Bunch liked to hide out when they were running from the law. It's no wonder when you take into account the park's landscape, which is highlighted by canyons, buttes and high, reef-like ridgelines.

The Waterpocket Fold is the park's primary attraction. This 100-mile-long fold in the Earth's crust is riddled with basins and small pockets that trap millions of gallons of rainwater each year, influencing the region's flora and fauna in the process.

The historic settlement of Fruita, near the middle of the park, is certainly worth a visit. It's surrounded by

the Calf Creek Recreation Area. You'll see the path at the far end of the camping area. It's the only maintained trail nearby.

For more information, call 435-826-5499 or log onto http://ut.blm.gov/monument.

orchards that were planted at the end of the 19th century and the trees still produce fruit.

Likely of more interest to children is the one-room schoolhouse, built in 1897 and used until 1941. Even if there's no one around to open the doors, you can easily

The intriguing landscape of Goblin Valley State Park

peer in the windows and see everything on display — just as it once was used. For our kids, this peek into the past was the subject of conversation for days.

There are 15 day hikes in the Fruita area alone, as well as several overnight ones. Some are strenuous and climb high above the valley floor, but others are quite easy. Rather than list them all here, we recommend that you stop by the visitor center to obtain a map and ask for up-to-date trail advice.

Other adventure activities are somewhat limited. As in most other national parks, mountain biking is restricted to designated roads and rock climbing is not well-developed, owing to the predominance of soft, flaky sandstone.

For more information, call 435-425-3791 or log onto www.nps.gov/care.

Goblin Valley State Park

Although located in "the middle of nowhere", Goblin Valley State Park is a great destination if you have the time to explore it, especially with kids. The "goblins" are curiously shaped sand and mudstone pillars situated in an unusual valley setting. They have names that were apparently devised just for kids: Kermit the Frog and Porky Pig are two that come to mind.

The movie Galaxy Quest was filmed at Goblin Valley State Park, owing to the "out of this world" scenery. There's a great little campsite here that's used mainly by local residents, so it's rarely crowded. Spending the night amongst a host of goblins may seem a little spooky, but the kids will love it.

A marked, informative nature trail leads through several bizarre formations near the campground. It doesn't take long to walk it and it's guaranteed to excite even road-weary youngsters.

Goblin Valley State Park is best approached from Highway 24, with an access point located 19.5 miles north of Hanksville. Head west for five miles on the paved road (watch for the directional signs) and then drive south for seven miles on the gravel road. If you're driving a 4x4 vehicle, you'll be happy to learn that there are lots of great off-road driving opportunities nearby. (Check with the park staff at the campground entrance for suggestions.)

The intriguing landscape of Goblin Valley State Park

Kanab

Travel times to:

Las Vegas: via Highway 89 (north), Highway 9 (west), Highway 15 (south); 3½ hours
Salt Lake City: via Highway 89 (north), Highway 70 (west), Highway 15 (north); 5½ hours
Zion National Park: via Highway 89 (north), Highway 9 (west); 45 minutes
Bryce Canyon: via Highway 89 (north), Highway 12 (east); 1½ hours
Coral Pink Sand Dunes: via Highway 89 (north), Hancock Road, Sand Dunes Road; 45 minutes

Lake Powell

It's a huge lake, measuring 186 miles from Glen Canyon to the furthest northeast shore.

as a
base

Lake Powell was created when a portion of the Colorado River Valley was flooded after the completion of the Glen Canyon Dam in 1966. It offers incredibly striking vistas and is one of the most intriguing places to go boating in the United States.

It's a huge lake, measuring 186 miles from Glen Canyon to the furthest northeast shore. Ninety-six tentacles of water reach into what were once arid canyons and "washes" along the way. If you count up all the inlets, the length of Lake Powell's shoreline totals a staggering 1,960 miles — longer than the entire west coast of the United States!

Simply put, houseboating is the best way to enjoy Lake Powell. Because of its sheer size, a few day trips are inadequate to explore all that it has to offer. Camping overnight along the lakeshore, with the cries of wild donkeys and coyotes literally on your doorstep, is a magical experience and one that kids will especially love. We recommend giving yourself at least three nights out on the lake on a houseboat, or even more if you can manage it.

It's not just the boating experience that makes Lake Powell so exciting. Dozens of archeological sites are located near the lakeshore or pocketed in canyons that rise above the water. Any one of

them will provide a fantastic chance to explore the beautiful surrounding landscape, which is not accessed as easily by land routes. In fact, almost any hike up from the lakeshore can be incredibly rewarding.

This is an adventure you'll probably want to undertake sooner rather than later. The creation of Lake Powell has long been controversial. The construction of the Glen Canyon Dam and the subsequent flooding that created Lake Powell was also partly responsible for the birth of the modern environmental movement. A campaign to drain Lake Powell and restore the lakebed to its natural state has gained much momentum in recent years. While it's unlikely that the lake will be drained soon — if ever — boating activities might face more restrictions in the coming years.

Try to avoid visiting the lake during the summer months of July and August. Boat traffic is much busier then and the rental rates for houseboats are also higher. Availability might be an issue in the summer, too, so phoning the Wahweap Marina (928-645-2433 or 800-528-6154) to reserve a boat is always a good idea. May, June, September and October are particularly good months for houseboating, as well as April and November if the weather conditions remain stable and warm.

One of the most interesting aspects of the "houseboat adventure" is learning how to maneuver the craft if you've never done so before. After you check in at the marina, you'll be given a quick but thorough "crash course" on your new boat, its attributes and things you must be aware

of while piloting it. Pay close attention to the instructions on docking, reversing and securing the boat alongside a beach area — you'll need to understand these techniques for your overnight stays down the lake.

Once you have enough groceries, water, firewood and fuel stowed on board to last the entire length of your intended trip, then cast off! You'll first cross the rather wide Wahweap Bay and Warm Creek Bay to reach a narrower channel, which then widens out again into Padre Bay and Last Chance Bay.

Depending on the time of day, you might want to look for your first campsite in this area. Alternatively, keep moving to reach

better sites further up the lake. (Ask marina personnel for advice concerning the best camping spots; they will vary depending on the lake's water level and the time of year.) Although there's no shortage of good sites, you won't want to try to moor the boat along a steep or unstable shoreline after nightfall.

About a third of the way up the navigable part of the lake (at least with a large houseboat) is the Dangling Rope Marina. This is a great place to stock up on supplies that may have been forgotten, empty the sewage tank, refuel or even send a postcard! See if the kids can spot some of the giant carp that usually swim below the marina's dock.

From this point on, all that should limit your lake adventure is the time you have available. Rainbow Bridge National Monument is a worthwhile hiking goal — if you can find it — but almost any other "up-lake" destination will be nearly as exciting. Bon voyage!

Page

Although there's little in Page to interest most visitors, it's a good starting point to set off with a rented houseboat (see previous section). You can also embark on an overland journey from here, whether it's to Monument Valley, Lee's Ferry or places that are even more remote. The town has a number of well-stocked stores and lots of restaurants, motels and gas stations.

While you're in Page, why not try to arrange a tour of the Glen Canyon Dam? Your kids will probably find it fascinating. Tours gen-erally operate four times per day throughout most of the year. Be sure to phone ahead to arrange your tour, at 928-608-6404.

Even if you don't book a tour of the dam, try to stop by the Carl Hayden Visitor Center to check out its informative exhibits, watch a short film or perhaps buy a souvenir or two. The center is open every day (except Christmas Day, Thanksgiving Day and New Year's Day.)

Moab

The rugged desert landscape around Moab, with its towering red pinnacles and hidden canyons, is like an invitation to the ultimate game of hide and go seek.

as a base

As Mecca is to Muslims, Moab is to mountain bikers. And Slickrock Trail is the Holy Grail. For the spokes and shocks set, this town of 5,000 in southeastern Utah has been a pilgrimage for many years.

What not as many people realize, though, is that there is a wealth of other adventures in this area too - especially for families. From hiking to the "Delicate Arch" (see Arches/Canyonlands chapter), or rafting the not-always-delicate whitewater of the Colorado River, Moab has enough natural delights to keep you satisfied for years..

Of course you won't have been the first to do so. The town was first settled in 1855 by Mormons who were forced away after running afoul of native inhabitants. By 1876, Mormons were back to stay. Since then the town has been a hub for everything from fruit growing to uranium production. Today, tourism is by far and away the most important sector of the economy.

Biking Moab's famous Slickrock trail

American Southwest

Camping around Moab

If you are camping while in Moab, don't be discouraged if all the local campgrounds are full (and they often are). There is a free alternative that - while not providing amenities like showers - will afford you amazing views, no traffic noise, and lots of space for the kids to roam.

These are the Bureau of Land Management areas designated for overnight use. There are oodles of them around Moab. One of our favorites is along the Horsethief Road. To get there, drive north of Moab on Hwy 191 for about 10 miles, and then west towards Canyonlands National Park on Hwy 313 about 15 miles further. The campsite is on your right, near a sign marking Horsethief Road.

What you'll find when you get there is about two dozen nice spots to camp, set alongside a gravel covered ring road, in the middle of which is a large field of wild grasses. The view is spectacular, with sagebrush covered desert in front and layer upon layer of hills, from craggy looking bluffs to the high peaks of the La Sal Range fading into the distance. Looking out from the camping area to the left are sheer-faced red mesas and to the right, rolling open country.

Most of the camping spots have rustic fire pits set up by previous overnighters. If you've got mountain bikes with you, there are plenty of places to pedal around in the immediate vicinity. Look also for several other areas to camp off the side of Dead Horse Road.

There are also a few campsites to choose from along the Colorado River, quite close to town. Because of their proximity though, they get filled-up quickly and are also a bit on the noisy side, being just off the side of the road.

Its world-famous mountain biking has created a bit of a scene around Moab, at least for part of the year. ATV's, Hum-V's and dirt bikes buzz around the same red rock bluffs that bikers and hikers enjoy. Jet boats rocket down the same waterways that provide such excellent canoeing and kayaking opportunities nearby.

There are trendy cafes, microbreweries and outdoor gear shops all over the main drag,

Calm water on the Colorado River, where floating along is a pure pleasure

but there are also decent places to do your grocery shopping. The excellent visitor's information centre will help equip you to get out of town and explore in more peace.

For accommodation, dozens of motels, bed and breakfasts, and apartments are available to choose from. There's also a few RV parks, many state campgrounds and oodles of free places to pitch a tent on the Bureau of Land Management territory surrounding town (see box below). Ask for directions at the information center.

High season is April to June and October. If you'd like to drop paddle on the Colorado or Green Rivers, come before October, when water levels are too low for most boating opportunities.

Paved walking trails throughout town allow you to walk and bike, whilst in the middle of all the action. If you don't have a vehicle, shuttles can be arranged to many of the trailheads on the outskirts of town (check

at the info center).

The following itineraries and activities will help your family get the most out of Moab.

Moab Visitor Information Center: 435-259-8825

Activities in the Moab Area:

Moab Rim Adventure Park

This park on the far north side of town has a little bit of everything. There's a chairlift, hiking trails, a downhill mountain bike park, rappelling, guided cave tours and a climbing wall, among other attractions. Located 1,000 feet above town, the park offers 360-degree views of the Moab area.

You can also see Anasazi rock art amongst the fin-shaped sandstone formations in the area. At nighttime, there's a Stargazing Deck with a high definition telescope, and an on-site astronomer to explain the different constellations.

for more info call: 435-259-7799

Float Trips on Green and Colorado Rivers

From May until October Moab is a hub for whitewater rafting, river kayaking and canoeing. Float trips Moab will take you through 320 million years of geologic history on the way through red rock canyons of the Colorado and Green rivers.

A number of rafting companies offer family-friendly trips - from a half-day itinerary to longer - in the Moab area. Most trips include some moderate whitewater, short hikes to see Native petroglyphs, and play time on sandy beaches. Sheri Griffith Expeditions (435-259-8229) and World Wide River Expeditions (1-800-231-2769) are two companies offering custom trips for kids as young as 5 years old.

Rock Climbing and Canyoneering

The rugged desert landscape around Moab, with its towering red pinnacles and hidden canyons, is like an invitation to the ultimate game of hide and go seek. Taking along some rock climbing equipment means you'll be ready to play. If you haven't got your rope, shoes and harness with you there are places to rent (Pagan Mountaineering 435-259-1117 and Gearheads 435-259-4327 are both in downtown Moab).

A few companies have introductory climb-

ing courses, and equipment rentals, for kids as young as five years old. Moab Cliffs and Canyons (435-259-3317) and Moab Desert Adventures (435-260-2404) both offer half-day to multi-day climbing trips.

Butch Cassidy's King World Water Park

This place is named after the famous out-law who holed up in the area after robbing banks (its pond is supposedly where Cassidy watered the horses and cattle he rustled).

The 17 acre park is a nice place to cool off on the hot summer days. It boasts 5 slides, 3 pools, paddle boats and sand volleyball among other attractions. Find it by driving 1.5 miles (2 km) north of downtown Moab on Highway #191. Turn right just past the large Waterpark sign.

for more info call: 435-259-2837

Highways 128 & 279: Colorado River

These roads, both of which start a mile or two from US 191 north of Moab, are fabulous for their canyon views, their picnic stops, and their range of activities. Perhaps Moab's best known rock climbing area – "Wall Street" – is just a few miles south on #279 (you can't miss it!). Several short hikes from both roads lead to natural arches and other interesting formations.

Probably our best advice to families with loose schedules is simply to amble along and discover at will. If the weather's hot, there's always a refreshing wade close at hand (that being said, watch the current along this stretch of the Colorado River, especially in spring: it's generally faster than you might think).

Itineraries

1 | Slickrock Practise Loop

Distance: 2 miles
Time: 1/2 hour
Difficulty: Moderate

The Slickrock practice loop offers the ulti-

The practice loop provides a good introduction to Slick-rock riding

mate way to get a taste of Moab's famous slickrock riding, and to warm up for the longer and tougher realities of the Slickrock Trail proper. We highly recommend that you and your kids give the practice loop a go before committing its far more demanding cousin.

If you haven't brought bikes with you, it's easy – if a little expensive – to rent them in Moab. See gear shop options in our Appendix section at the back of this book for contacts, or shop around in Moab once you've arrived to find the best gear at the best prices.

Both circuits start from the same place. From Downtown Moab turn eastwards on 300 South, turn right at the road's end and then turn left at the second street you come to (this turn-off is well signed). Follow Sand Flats Road beyond to a fee station (everyone must pay), and then about 0.6 mile further. Just beyond the Slickrock campsite you'll see a rather large and paved parking area on the left side, with toilets (but no water). Park here.

The trailhead is obvious, at the north end of the parking area. Mount your bikes after quickly negotiating a gate and sandy wash, then follow white "pavement" markers on a circuitous routing for about 0.5 miles. Here you'll see a sign indicating the practice loop (to your right), vs. Slickrock itself.

The rest of the route is self-explanatory. Stay the course of white markers as they continue northwards and above most of the surrounding rocks, then drop in a winding fashion towards the well named "Abyss". Here you'll see a minor deviation to Negro Bill Canyon outlook; the view is great and takes only a few minutes to cycle towards (bear in mind that you will have to climb a

few feet on your way back).

Final stretches of the practice loop, before it rejoins the main trail, negotiate several sandy washes as well as relatively steep rocky grades. These are typical of what you'll encounter on the Slickrock Trail – but easier! (Thought we'd warn you…).

Once you rejoin the practice loop, you have the option of returning to your car (left) or heading right to try a mile or two of Slickrock. This isn't a bad option if you have lots of energy, water and snacks. Remember, though, as you look down this stretch of Slickrock, that it will be uphill for awhile coming back.

2 Slickrock Main Loop

Distance: 10.6 miles
Time: 2 – 4 hours
Difficulty: Difficult

The word "slickrock" was coined by early settlers, whose horses had difficulty crossing sandstone slabs with metal-shod hooves. Modern mountain bikers experience exactly the opposite thing: this gritty rock offers incredible traction (at least when it's dry), meaning that steep descents and ascents are often surprisingly do-able.

Our description of the Slickrock Loop below is not very comprehensive, chiefly because on two successive attempts we were unable to complete it (the first time out one bike broke down completely; on the second it was heat exhaustion that did our 10 year old in, albeit after he'd nearly made it to the half way point).

There is lots of good – and inexpensive – literature describing the whole loop though, should you determine to try it. Keep our experience in mind while doing so: if breakdowns occur, whether mechanical or human, you can always retrace your steps to the starting point. Thus, the length and apparent commitment of the Loop shouldn't hold you back.

The technical difficulty of the Slickrock route should give you cause for concern though, which is why we recommend biking the practice loop first (see above). Begin the Loop as described for this, staying left at signs indicating it. Descend gradually over several sandstone bluffs at first – controlling speed carefully as you go – to a junction that splits the Loop (about 3.5 miles along).

Stunning scenery and great riding along the Slickrock main loop

No matter which way you go, you'll arrive back at this junction later on. It is supposedly easier to trend left (south) here though, and return via the north leg. If you do follow this routing, you'll pass Natural Selection Point, Portal View, Overlook and nearby the so-called Shrimp Rock before rejoining the approach route.

Take plenty of water and snacks. Don't forget to pack spares, a pump and repair kit too – otherwise, you might be in for a long walk in the sun!

3 Mill Canyon Dinosaur Trail

Distance: ¼ mile
Time: ½ hour
Difficulty: Easy

Trying to find this trail is half the fun. To get here, take Highway 191 north of Moab for about 15 miles until you see a sign on left side of road for Mill Canyon. Cross over the train tracks and pass a parking area on your immediate right.

Continue along the rough dirt road until you see an old brown sign. Turn left towards Mill Canyon. About 0.6 mile along is a sign for "Halfway Stage Station". Turn right at it.

Another 0.6 mile along a heavily rutted road is a sign on the right for the "Dinosaur Trail". The trail starts behind the registration box and is just a ¼ mile in length.

This trail is like an outdoor paleontological museum. The self-guided path contains 150 million year old skeletal remains of numerous kinds of dinosaurs including: Allosaurus, camptosaurus and Stegosaurus.

The dino bones are a little difficult to spot at first. Go across the creek and up a trail onto the far ridge. The bones are a dark-brownish color and are embedded in the sandstone cliffs. The bones are out in the open, so touching them is permitted.

The fossils are marked by some old dilapidating wooden stakes with numbers that are visible, but barely. The most interesting fossils are the tail at #7 and part of a spine at #9.

4 Biking the Gemini Bridges Trail

Distance: 14 miles (from US 313 to US 191)
Time: 1 ½ to 3 hours
Difficulty: Moderate

This is an easy and fun ride of 14 miles or so, the highlight of which are the Gemini Bridges themselves, massive rock arches that you can actually ride on top of! There's only one gradual uphill section (around the 10 mile mark); much of the rest is a downwards glide.

The best way to tackle it is to either have someone shuttle you and the kids to the upper trailhead (a shuttle service is available in Moab during biking season. Park a car down at the exit, or have a designated driver who can bring you up and wait down below.)

We'd recommend starting this ride early in the day, especially if the weather is going to be warm. The middle and latter sections are often particularly hot. Take lots of water, snacks and a camera for the bridges.

From Moab, drive north on Hwy 191 for about 12 miles to its

junction with Hwy 313. Turn left and drive about 13 miles further in the direction of Dead Horse Point. A short distance past roadside marker 10, you'll see the Gemini Bridges trail sign on your left side. Park here.

The distance to the bridges is about 5 1/2 miles, on a jeep road with lots of signage to keep you on track. The first 4 miles or so is an especially fast downhill,

Easy but fun riding along the Gemini Bridges trail

along which you'll spot a number of great places to camp.

Since the bridges are the highlight of the trip, take some time there to explore around them and on the peninsula of rock beyond. It goes without saying that young kids have to watched very carefully here: any slip from the top would be catastrophic. Look for some climbers' bolts at the top of a very overhanging - and scary - face near one bridge.

To resume travel, walk or ride your bike up and left until you regain the well traveled descent path. Wind down, and then down some more on a wide track with lots of signs confirming that you're still on route (it's hard to go wrong along it in any event). A steeper descent brings you to a junction about 9 miles into the trip. Turn left here and follow signs for highway 101.

The only real climb begins past a narrow opening in the cliffs ahead. Settle into a good pace for tackling it with kids, particularly if it's hot. We found that a rest stop, with snacks and water, was pretty essential about 10 minutes into it or so.

The final section of road thankfully drops a fair distance before it reaches a large parking area off Highway 191 (about 1 mile south of the junction with #313). If your ride is waiting here, then you'll be out of the saddle in no time. If not, there's still about 11 miles of pavement between you and Moab.

Moab

Travel times to:

Salt Lake City: via #191 Hwy (north), #6 Hwy (north), 4 1/2 hours.
Grand Junction: via #191 Hwy (north), #70 (east), 2 hours
Monument Valley: via #191 Hwy (south), #163 (east), 3 1/2 hours.
Arches National Park: via #191 Hwy (north), 10 minutes.
Canyonlands National Park: via #191 Hwy (north). #313 (south), 1 hour.

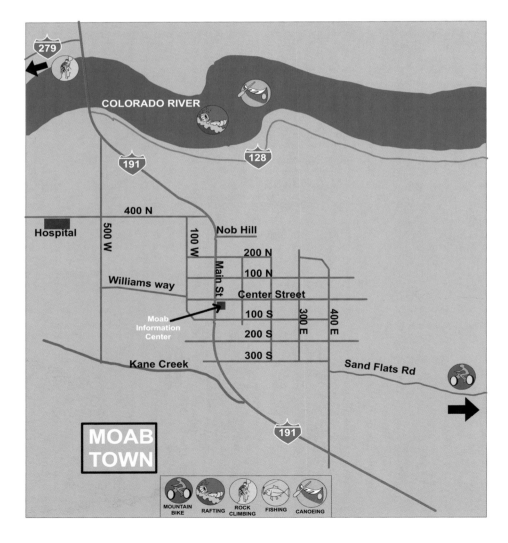

Arches National Park & Canyonlands National Park

Canyonlands remains one of the least disturbed natural regions of the Colorado Plateau

as a base

Although relatively small (at less than 80,000 acres in size), Arches National Park has some of the most stunning "red rock" desert scenery in the Southwest. Of course, the 2,000 sandstone arches located within it are the most spectacular geological features. Perhaps more exquisite than any other, Delicate Arch constitutes one of America's most familiar and beloved natural landscapes.

Canyonlands National Park, on the other hand, is comprised of a fantastic agglomeration of canyons, mesas and buttes within a much larger land area (338,000 acres). The Colorado River and the Green River merge here in a very dramatic and impressive fash-

Arches National Park and Canyonlands National Park just beg to be explored

ion. Canyonlands remains one of the least disturbed natural regions of the Colorado Plateau and therefore rewards modern travelers with a tantalizing glimpse of how the entire area must have appeared before the encroachment of humans.

People have been visiting Arches and Canyonlands for over 10,000 years, roughly from the end of the last ice age. The primary motivation for the earliest incursions was likely the desire to obtain rocks for making tools, with hunting and gathering activities probably following shortly afterwards. There is also evidence suggesting more esoteric pursuits; the deep canyons and unusual rock formations have long made this place spiritually significant for native people.

In addition to the hoards of human visitors during the summer months, modern inhabitants of both parks include many of the same animal species found elsewhere in the Southwest's deserts. Arches is one of two places we've seen rattlesnakes on our many desert explorations. If our experience is anything to go by, the local snake population is a healthy one.

Stop by the visitor center of either park to learn more about the area's fascinating natural and human history. The centers, as with all such facilities in the United States' national park system, offer great insights for exploring the landscape in detail and they also provide up-to-date information on trail conditions.

Arches National Park

In addition to the intriguing rock formations that give the park its name, Arches' sandstone landscape is chock full of other interesting features. Delicately balanced rocks, fins and pinnacles are just some of the striking landforms that can be seen throughout the park.

What's with all the Arches?

Weird geology makes for cool sandstone shapes at Arches National Park

The best way to reach them is on foot, although some can be accessed by car alone. This section details some of the more interesting and pleasant walks we've discovered in Arches. Most are relatively short and can be completed within half a day, or less. If you have the time (and the inclination), try some other routes, too. Park personnel will give you all the pointers you need to choose the ones that are most appropriate for kids.

To really experience Arches National Park to the fullest, camping out for a night or two is an absolute must. The Devil's Garden campground is one of the nicest campsites we can think of, with spacious sites scattered amidst beautiful red rocks. You're a long way from a main road here, so the campground also provides an absolutely breathtaking sense of peace. Several good hikes and rock climbs can be found nearby (see below) and park staff offer daily interpretive shows at the foot of one of the park's arches.

Campsites are available on a "first come, first serve" basis and stays can be arranged at the visitor center by the park gates off Highway 191. Get there as early in the day as you can (i.e. before 9 a.m. during the high season - spring thru early autumn).

To find Arches National Park, take Highway 191 and drive five miles north of Moab. Go through the park entrance and continue for another 18 miles to Devil's Garden at the road's end.

Arches National Park Junior Ranger Program

While parents are enjoying the park's spectacular scenery, kids can get busy learning about it. Go to the Arches National Park Visitor Center (located five miles north

midday heat. Finally, the late-afternoon light on the arch accentuates its beauty, which is revealed in stunning shades of gold. It's an experience you won't soon forget.

The hike starts at the Wolfe Ranch parking area, located about 13 miles from the park entrance and seven miles from the Devil's Garden campground. Within a few hundred yards of the parking area, a side route leads to some extremely well-preserved petroglyphs (rock drawings) to the left of the trail. It's worth taking the time to explore this area, especially if your children haven't had much first-hand exposure to native drawings before.

of Moab, off Highway 191) and pick up a children's activity booklet. It contains word games, fill-in-the-blank questions and fun facts about the geological formations and wildlife found in the park.

To earn their "Ranger" badges, kids will be expected to watch a slide show at the visitor center and collect a bag full of litter or empty pop cans.

For more information, call 435-719-2299.

After about half a mile, the well-defined trail ends and the route continues up a slick expanse of rock (clearly marked with a series of rock cairns). Although the climb is gradual through this section, it is exposed to the sun, so take lots of water breaks as you go.

1 Hike to Delicate Arch

Distance: 3 miles (round trip)
Time: 2 to 3 hours
Difficulty: Moderate (includes a 500-foot climb and descent)

This hike's biggest reward is a view of one of the world's most spectacular natural arches. We recommend starting out a couple of hours before sunset, for several reasons. Firstly, the crowds tend to diminish as daylight fades. Secondly, the kids (and you) will be spared the

The path levels out at the top of a broad

Petroglyphs near the Delicate Arch trail

An evening stroll along the Delicate Arch trail

escarpment that features pretty stands of juniper trees, and then follows a narrow rock ledge for about 200 yards. Your kids will enjoy squeezing along this narrow defile and you'll all love how it ends on a ridge crest overlooking Delicate Arch, situated about 100 yards away.

The rock slabs below the arch are perfect places to have a picnic, take some photographs or just absorb the fabulous view. Once you've had your fill, head back the way you came.

2 Hike to Landscape Arch

Distance: 2 miles (round trip)
Time: 45 minutes to 1½ hours
Difficulty: Easy

This is a nice, short hike that's easily accessed from the Devil's Garden campground. We recommend starting out early in the morning, before the crowds of day visitors have had a chance to make the 18-mile drive to this end of the park. That way, you'll likely only be joined on the trail by fellow campers.

Start from the Devil's Garden trailhead parking area (approximately 300 yards from the campground entrance) and follow a flat, gravel path. About 100 yards up the trail and off to the left, you'll see a ramp of sand wedged between two rock walls. If your kids are anything like ours, they'll love climbing up and running down it.

The spectacular span of Landscape Arch

The enormous span of Landscape Arch.

becomes visible on the left shortly afterwards. With a total span distance greater than the length of a football field, it's an awesome spectacle.

If you and your kids feel like continuing the hike, short side trips lead to Tunnel Arch or Pine Tree Arch. If not, just return the way you came.

3 Arches Campsite Ridge Walk

Distance: ½ mile
Time: 1-2 hours
Difficulty: Moderate to Difficult (climbing ability is required)

The sandstone ridges near the Arches Campsite just beg to be scrambled along and all offer great views of the surrounding area. Some are relatively long (over 500 yards), but are easily traversed. Most are not continuous, however, and climbing is made more difficult by the presence of steep (and often loose) rock steps, which demand that hikers pay close attention to the terrain.

One of the ridges is readily accessible from Campsite 6 through Campsite 12. Simply walk a few feet west, scramble up some easy slabs and you'll soon be at the top. Don't allow kids to climb up unattended, however. The west side of the ridge has a vertical drop of nearly 75 feet.

While this ridge climb is easy to get to and worth a quick trip, another ridge, accessed from near Campsite 21, is far more interesting and provides fantastic views of the surrounding desert landscape — including nearby Skyline Arch.

You'll need to have some climbing ability to

overcome a few short but tough sections of trail. We'd recommend attempting it only once the kids have been roped up, since there are a couple of sections where poten-tially nasty falls could occur.

Canyonlands National Park

The Colorado River and the Green River divide Canyonlands National Park into four districts: the Island in the Sky, the Needles, the Maze and the Rivers. They share some similarities, but each of them also has its own intriguing and unique characteristics.

The Island in the Sky district occupies a high mesa that offers a 180º view overlooking the Green River and Colorado River canyons. Its altitude allows quick and easy access to other high vantage points. There's also a spectacular camping area (the Willow Flats Campground, with 12 rustic sites), as well as several worthwhile hikes and the starting point for the Schafer Road descent (see below).

The Maze represents "canyon country" at

Swordfighting above the Green River in Canyonlands National Park

its finest. With a topography of steep-walled canyons, it is the least accessible of the four Canyonlands districts. You'll need lots of time, and almost certainly a four-wheel-drive vehicle, to tackle the rugged terrain of the Maze.

With colorful sandstone spires dominating its landscape, the Needles district occupies the southeast corner of the park. Popular as a climbing and backpacking destination, it's best accessed from Highway 191, south of Moab.

The Colorado River and Green River merge near the center of Canyonlands National Park. Beyond this junction is Cataract Canyon — a stretch of incredibly turbulent water famous amongst whitewater paddlers around the world. Above the canyon, however, both rivers are tranquil and offer canoeists and kayakers relaxing excursions.

Hiking and biking

Canyonlands National Park is a great place to hike and bike. There are too many good routes to be covered adequately in these pages, so we'd advise that you stop by one of the park's visitor centers to gather information on suitable hiking and biking

trails before setting out.

That being said, here are a couple of pointers that might make your planning a little easier. Most of the park's best shorter hikes are in the Island in the Sky district, while longer backpacking routes tend to begin in the Needles district. (Please note that you'll need a permit to camp anywhere in the park.)

Canyonlands is well-known as a mountain biking destination. The Schafer Road route (see below) and the 100-mile White Rim Road are both great for single-day or multiple-day trips. Be aware, however, that bikers are required to stay on designated roads in all areas of the park.

1　Schafer Road Descent

Distance: 10 miles (to Potash)
Time: 2 hours
Difficulty: Moderate

Have you ever biked 2,000 feet down into a canyon? That's exactly what the Schafer Road lets you do. From a high point of about 6,000 feet near the Canyonlands National Park entry gate and visitor center, the road snakes its way down to a point just above the Colorado River, at around 4,000 feet. It's

a spectacular descent, albeit a little bumpy at times.

The great thing about this route is that your vehicle can travel alongside the bikers in your group, meaning that cyclists don't have to carry water, snacks or tool kits on the way down. Because of this ongoing "roadside assistance", your kids only have to bike for as long as they like. Switching drivers is just a matter of pulling over to the side of the road for a few moments.

Highway 279 is paved and connects with the dirt descent track at Potash, about 15 miles from Moab. The entire route can be covered by bike, but your kids may want to hop off their saddles at the start of the paved section.

Winding down Schafer Road

There's significant vehicle traffic on this route, so camping (unfortunately) is not permitted until well past the park boundary, near a potash mine located about seven miles down. From this point, a few tracks lead to some

primitive campsites, which are worthwhile staying at if you've brought your gear along anyway and want to break up the descent over several days.

Along the way, consult the map that came with your park pass (or pick up a better one in Moab). From the trailhead half a mile north of the Canyonlands National Park Visitor Center, the route starts off easily and almost level as it contours around the upper walls of the canyon. The real drop begins after about 15 minutes of cycling. You'll have to switchback down 1,000 feet of steep

dirt track, watching carefully for vehicles grinding their way up and staying alert for loose surfaces that could cause a slip.

A junction at the end of this initial drop separates your road (heading to the left) from one that continues along the White Rim area straight ahead. Continue the descent, which is no longer as steep and alternates between the sides of a beautiful, red rock canyon. A sign a little further on marks the eastern boundary of the park and you'll soon come to the edge of a steep, 500-foot drop to the Colorado River. It's a spectacular view, with the Gooseneck Loop of the Colorado River right below.

At this point, you are almost exactly below Dead Horse Point State Park (see below). You might be able to see people waving from the top end of the park or hear their voices if the air is calm enough.

From here, the track gently climbs and descends on the raised river bank, eventually heading away from the Colorado River and into the mining district of Potash. It ends (almost too quickly) at the extreme southern end of Highway 279. From there, it's about 15 miles to Moab.

Near Canyonlands

Dead Horse Point State Park

This is a fantastic park in its own right and practically adjoins the Islands in the Sky district of Canyonlands National Park. Possibly its single best feature is the campsite, which sits right on top of a 2000-foot cliff above the Colorado River. From it, you can look straight down at the Gooseneck Loop — a perfect 180º bend in the river.

Dead Horse Point Park has an interesting history, even if it's rather sad. During the late 1800s, it was used as a natural corral by local cowboys. Wild horses were driven through a 30-yard-wide neck of land encompassed by fences, with sheer cliffs on all of the other sides. Here, the horses were roped and broken, with the best ones selected for sale to eastern markets.

Any unwanted horses (known as "broomtails") would be left to find their own way off the narrow point of land, although a gate in the fence was left open to assist them. On one occasion, however, a small herd of broomtails didn't leave — for reasons that are still unclear — and they all died of thirst.

This sad story does offer one important lesson to modern visitors to the park. There are no natural sources of water, so camping out without stocking up on water ahead of time could be a very thirsty experience.

MesaVerde National Park

The archeological remains in Mesa Verde are some of the best-preserved sites in the United States.

The ancient cliff dwellings at Mesa Verde (Spanish for "green table") are unrivaled in America's Southwest. Visitors to this spectacular park will get a close-up look at one of North America's most fascinating aboriginal cultures, with the whole place feeling like an open-air museum. Even a small amount of time spent here will be deeply memorable, especially for kids.

The culture on display at Mesa Verde is between 800 and 1,400 years old. For 600 or 700 years, it flourished and eventually led to the construction of cliff dwellings. Elaborate stone villages were built in sheltered alcoves in the canyon walls in about the last 100 years of human occupation. Archeologists have unearthed over 600 such dwellings in the Mesa Verde area.

Extended drought conditions eventually forced the inhabitants of the cliff dwellings

Mesa Verde's cliff dwellings are among the best-preserved aboriginal sites in North America

Driving and staying in the park

Roadside pullouts in Mesa Verde offer views such as these

It's quite a long and circuitous drive through Mesa Verde National Park, from the entrance gates off Highway 160 to where the road ends at the Ute Mountain Reservation. To keep your kids interested in the area during an extended stay, you might want to check out some of the nearby lodging or camping options.

The Morefield Village Campground, located four miles from the park entrance, is a good option for an overnight stay if you've brought camping gear along. It's also the only campground within the park. There are lots of spaces for tents and RVs, plus hot showers, laundry facilities and a nice trail through a recent burn area to the northwest. (Just ask the campground staff for directions.)

If you're not traveling with camping gear, consider staying at the Far View Lodge, near the Far View Visitor Center. The amenities are nice, meals are available at the Terrace restaurant (¼ of a mile away) and the vistas are absolutely superb. Phone 1-800-449-2288 for more information or to book rooms.

to move to areas with more reliable water supplies. Mesa Verde was deserted, with the cliff dwellings and various artifacts (such as tools and pottery) the only remaining evidence of their stay here.

The archeological remains in Mesa Verde are some of the best-preserved sites in the United States. The park service has done a commendable job of making them accessible to visitors — especially families — through a series of short paths and well-placed vantage points.

Try to spend at least a day or two here if you can. A trip to the Southwest that bypasses this place is akin to skipping a visit to the pyramids of Giza on a trip to Egypt. The park entrance is nine miles east of Cortez (see description below) and 35 miles west of Durango, Colorado, on Highway 160.

You can get a great view of the Cliff Palace from above or take a tour to the ruin itself

Mesa Verde Cliff Palace

The Mesa Verde Cliff Palace is about two miles past the Far View Visitor Center on the long and winding road that runs through Mesa Verde National Park. It is perhaps the most impressive example of any Anastazi Indian mountainside community.

Rediscovered in the 1880s by a couple of local cowboys, archeologists determined that the Cliff Palace was the main center of this civilization and it's been dated to at least 1100 AD. To view it up close, you'll have to go with a guide. You can make arrangements (and payment) for one at the visitor center.

Alternatively, it's possible to get a decent look at the Cliff Palace from the railed-in overlook that's perched above it. Try to catch what guides are telling nearby tour groups on the platform if you want a free description.

Balcony House

The one-hour Balcony House tour is the most challenging in Mesa Verde National Park and thus will be exciting for kids and parents alike. You have to descend 100 steps into the canyon, climb a 32-foot-long ladder, crawl through a 12-foot-long tunnel and then climb up another 60 feet of ladders and stone steps. We highly recommend it! (Inquire about this tour and others at the visitor center.)

An alternative to the tour is walking down a ¾-mile-long pathway to an overlook. If you've already checked out the Cliff Palace from its roadside overlook, however, this view of Balcony House will probably be a bit disappointing.

Spruce Tree House

Spruce Tree House is Mesa Verde's best-preserved dwelling and — refreshingly— you don't have to buy tickets to see it. You will have to undertake a ½-mile walk, but it's definitely worth the effort. Once there, kids and adults will get a clearer understanding of how the Anastazi lived. Be sure to pick up an interpretive brochure beforehand from the museum located at the trailhead.

Particularly interesting for the kids will be a climb down a ladder into a small enclosure (No. 6 in the brochure). The space is somewhat dark and mysterious, and is where the tribe performed healing ceremonies.

It's a good idea to get to Spruce Tree House early in the day, since it can become crowded later on. If your kids still have energy to burn after exploring the site, keep walking along the Petroglyph Trail (see below).

Mesa Verde Museum

Designated as a World Heritage Site by the United Nations in 1978, the Mesa Verde area is home to an impressive museum that was built in the 1930s. There are a number of interpretive displays of native history inside and descriptive films play every 30 minutes or so.

The hundreds of artifacts on display will be more interesting for the kids if they've seen either the Spruce Tree House or Cliff Palace beforehand. You might also want to visit the excellent on-site bookstore that documents every aspect of the Mesa Verde

Only the Spruce Tree House can be viewed at close range, independent of tour groups

culture.

Encourage the kids to participate in the junior ranger program at the museum. They'll be rewarded for learning about the area with a badge and a certificate.

1 Hiking the Petroglyph Loop

Distance: **2.8 miles**
Time: **1-2 hours**
Difficulty: **Easy**

The Petroglyph Loop trail is spectacular, interesting and fairly easy, which makes it ideal for kids. It's also the only trail in the park that gives visitors close-up views of petroglyphs. However, access to the trail is only permitted during the Spruce Tree House visiting hours. Confirm those times at the visitor center or with any park ranger.

Start the hike at the Spruce Tree House (see above). The narrow trail snakes its way between rocks and stands of juniper below the mesa rim, climbs for a short distance and then returns along a plateau to the park museum. Along the way, the route offers great views of Spruce Canyon and Navajo Canyon.

Cortez

as a
base

This town of 7,000 people in the southwest corner of Colorado was once called Tsaya-toh ("rock water") by the Navajo people. Cortez is beautifully situated between the mountains and the desert. As pretty as the setting is, it's Cortez's proximity to Mesa Verde National Park that makes it such a good base.

The park sits high atop a plateau nine miles out of town and offers an incredible look at America's pre-European past. Cliff dwellings that are 700 years old — from single houses to full villages — remain impressively intact, providing a fascinating glimpse into what life must have been like for ancestral Puebloans. (See the "Itineraries" section for more information.)

Morefield Village Campground (see above) is the only campground inside Mesa Verde National Park and is an excellent place for families to stay for a couple of days. Alternatively, there are a number of com-

mercial campgrounds located near the park entrance. If you'd rather sleep indoors, Cortez has a good selection of family-oriented motels and bed and breakfast places to choose from.

The town has a standard selection of fast food outlets and family restaurants. If your kids like Mexican food, your best bet is to forgo the more commercialized east end of town and try out one of the funky cantinas in the older downtown area.

Historically, Cortez residents have been heavily involved in farming and ranching. That tradition is showcased at annual events like the Ute Mountain Rodeo in June and the Montezuma County Fair in August. The townsite also served for eons as a major trading centre for both the Navajo and Ute people. Today, a strong Native American presence continues and is perhaps best expressed at the Cortez Cultural Centre (see below).

The peak tourist season is from June to September. Arriving a little before or a little after that period means you'll have your pick of campground sites and easy access to the town's amenities.

Listed below are some of our favorite family activities and itineraries in the area.

Activities in the Cortez area:

Reptile Reserve of Southern Colorado

This place is very cool and is home to about 150 rattlesnakes, four boa constrictors and two pythons — not to mention alligators and turtles. If you visit on a weekend between May and September, you might witness the animals' feeding time. The owners offer dozens of chicken sandwiches to the snakes (minus the bread, plus feathers). To get there, drive about five miles east of the Mesa Verde National Park entrance on Highway 160.

Parque de Vida

Located just off Main Street in Cortez, this park has a little bit of everything. There's a playground and skateboard park, as well as tennis, volleyball and basketball courts. If you've got a ball in the back of the car, dig it out and set the kids loose on one of the three multi-purpose playing fields.

For more information, call 970-565-3402.

Cortez Municipal Aquatics Complex

This is a good place for the kids to blow off some steam on a hot summer day. The highlight is a 125-foot, double-looped water slide. There's also a wading pool for younger kids. The facility is open daily between Memorial Day and Labor Day, and family rates are available.

For more information, call 970-565-7877.

Cortez

Travel times to:

Moab: via Highway 666 (north), Highway 191 (north); 2 hours and 15 minutes

Mesa Verde National Park: via Highway 160 (east); 10 minutes (to the park gates)

Monument Valley: via Highway 160 (west), Highway 191 (north), Highway 163 (west), Highway 42 (east); 3 hours

Canyon de Chelly National Monument: via Highway 160/666 (south), Highway 13 (west), Highway 63/68 (south); 3 hours

Santa Fe: via Highway 160/666 (south), Highway 64 (east), Highway 84 (south); 5 hours and 45 minutes

Navaho Nation

The massive red statues of rock that tower over this valley may be the most lasting image of the Southwest you take home with you.

The Navajo Nation of northeast Arizona (with smaller pieces of territory in Utah and New Mexico) is a sovereign native reserve, the largest of its kind in the United States. At 30,000 square miles, it is an enormous expanse of land by any measure.

A visit to the Southwest is just not complete without at least an introductory tour through the Navajo lands. Apart from their sweeping vistas and towering ramparts, your kids will get an inspirational view of this proud people. The modern Navajo way of life is at least partially representative of millennia-old customs and traditions, and this is an educational opportunity your children won't soon forget.

Thankfully, the Navajo people are generally quite welcoming to visitors on their soil, so long as certain rules are adhered to. These are not particularly onerous requirements, but they should be observed carefully and respectfully.

Try to fit an exploration of the Navajo Nation into your travel plans

Hot air ballooning over Monument Valley

Most importantly, people without Navajo ancestry are asked to not wander off established roads and trails, unless they have been given special permission. Visitors are also asked to not pick up or gather anything on Navajo land, nor deface the land or leave any visible scars. Finally, the drinking of alcohol is forbidden here.

Monument Valley

The massive "statues" of red rock that tower over Monument Valley may be the most lasting image of the Southwest that you'll take home with you. Chances are, they were already potent images in your mind before you even arrived.

Whether seen as caricatures in Bugs Bunny cartoons or as backdrops for western movies and car commercials on TV, the grandeur of these natural monuments will likely impress you more than any other landscape feature in the Southwest.

We suggest that you spend at least one night in Monument Valley to explore the area, even if you're only able to absorb a tiny fraction of its majestic beauty. Camping is the ultimate way to do that, at a spectacular site that overlooks the Mittens towers. If you haven't brought camping equipment with you, then staying in a nearby motel is a good alternative — at least for the easy access to this area that it offers.

Monument Valley can be approached either from the north or the south on Highway 163. The nearest settlement south of the valley is Kayenta. To the north, Mexican Hat is about an hour away. (See the "Southwest Highways" chapter for more information about driving through this region.)

If you're arriving from the south, you'll end up turning right just after you cross the state line into Utah. If you're driving down from the north, you'll know you've passed the

The Monument Valley Loop can be driven with an RV, albeit slowly

all-important turnoff if you find yourself in Arizona.

Look for the directional signs indicating Monument Valley. For about half a mile, this paved road climbs past roadside stands offering jewelry, Navajo fried foods and tacky souvenirs. It then continues on to a visitor center and campground.

The Monument Valley Navajo Tribal Park

Visitor's Center And Museum offers various Navajo wares, as well as information about interesting activities in the area. Note that anyone traveling through this area (nine years old and up) must pay an entry fee to get into the valley, even if it's just to use the campground.

Monument Valley Loop Drive

This awesome, 17-mile-long driving loop through the heart of Monument Valley is magnificent. Although it's fundamentally sound, the road leading into the valley is hard-packed with lots of potholes and bumps, so driving a larger vehicle (i.e. anything longer than 24 feet) is not recommended.

Traveling off the loop road is prohibited, since there are Navajo

Navajo Nation

Entering a traditional "hogan" in Monument Valley

At close to 30,000 square miles, the Navajo Reservation is the largest of its kind in the United States, encompassing parts of Arizona, Utah and New Mexico. The Navajo, who refer to themselves as Diné ("the people"), have become largely self-governing since forming the Navajo Tribal Government in 1923.

The Navajo population today numbers more than 210,000, a far cry from the 8,000 souls who survived the 1864 "Long Walk" and its aftermath. After the United States defeated Mexico in 1848, it took control of the present-day Southwest states. The U.S. government later moved to expel the Navajo people from their homeland. Colonel Kit Carson burned Navajo farms and communities to the ground and forced those who had not been killed to make the 300-mile trek to Fort Sumner, New Mexico. The Navajo were held in prison camps there and many perished. In 1868, a treaty was signed between the surviving Navajo and the U.S. government that allowed them to return to their land.

Over the past century, the Navajo have become more autonomous, although some still serve in the United States armed forces. During the Second World War, Navajo "codetalkers" devised the only code that wasn't broken by enemy intelligence experts. Today, many Navajo are proud members of the American military.

There are a number of famous sites to visit within the Navajo Reservation, including Monument Valley, Canyon de Chelly and Four Corners (the only place in the U.S. where four states converge at a single point).

Perhaps the best place to learn more about the Navajo people is the Navajo Nation Tribal Museum in Window Rock. This is the largest Native American museum in the country and features films, exhibits and displays that will give the whole family a better appreciation of the history and culture of the Navajo people.

Unbeatable tent sites overlook The Mittens

communities nearby. Mountain biking on the road is allowed, but the shoulders are almost non-existent and sometimes there's a fair bit of vehicle traffic. Should you choose not to drive this route on your own, guided tours in open-air vehicles can be booked at the visitor center.

Hot air ballooning is another popular activity that you can arrange at the visitor center. Those who don't take to the skies can still admire the colorful balloons while driving around.

The initial stretch of road descending from the visitor center contains the steepest grades of the entire loop, so if you can negotiate this section, you can manage anything else on the route. Watch for the "Three Sisters" formation a few miles along on the right. They consist of two thick pinnacles brooding over a thinner middle sister, and are reminiscent of Cinderella

and her cruel aunts. A little further along is John Ford's Point, which is home to Navajo sandstone dwellings and a place that offers horseback rides.

Further along is a spectacular view of the Totem Pole, a 300 foot freestanding pillar of rock whose base is barely thicker than its summit cap. In this area, you're likely to come across Navajo people selling turquoise jewelry and other handicrafts. We can think of no better place to do this kind of shopping.

Driving this loop at the posted speed limit of 10 miles per hour will take you about two hours to complete, not including rest stops.

When you return to the visitor center, take the kids to the Navajo Heritage Village located right next door. Here you'll find a sweat lodge (a ceremonial sauna of sorts), as well as female and male "hogans". These traditional structures are simple but beautiful, and are built primarily of logs and earth. You can go inside them and get a sense of what native ceremonies might have been like in centuries past. Interpretive plaques near the site explain what each facility was used for.

Accommodation

The campsite overlooking Monument Valley is truly outstanding. Two spots in particular allow you to peer out over the valley with unobstructed views. It's worth arriving early in the day to secure one of these sites. There are also a number of other beautifully situated spots for RVs or tent campers, with sheltered picnic tables, fire pits and impressive bathrooms (with showers). Winter camping rates are half what they are during the summer.

Canyon De Chelly National Monument

The Canyon de Chelly National Monument is unique among America's national parks and monuments, because it is comprised entirely of Navajo Tribal Trust land. A treasure trove of ancient artifacts, rock paintings and unique architecture, it is still home to a Navajo community.

For the Navajo, this place is infused with deep spiritual significance and great historical value. These qualities are apparent to the casual visitor as well, even if they're not as well understood.

Although it's a little off the beaten track, a trip to Canyon de Chelly is very worthwhile. This is especially true if you haven't visited (or won't be visiting) Mesa Verde in Colorado. Along with stunning canyon scenery, you'll get close-up views of ancient

Cave dwellings are close at hand in Canyon de Chelly

settlements such as the White House (see below) and gain a deeper understanding of how indigenous people have lived here over the centuries.

To get to Canyon de Chelly from Monument Valley, drive south on Highway 163 and then take Highway 191 to Chinle. (You can reach the same point by driving north on Highway 191 from Highway I 70, between Flagstaff and Albuquerque). From here, it's just a couple of miles east on Highway 7 to the park gates, the visitor center and the Cottonwood Campground.

Rim Drives

The best way to get a sense of the magnitude of this region is by driving along the South Rim Road or the North Rim Road. The former will take you to the parking area for the White House trail (see below)

and the Spider Rock Overlook. The latter runs past overlooks of two ancient ruins (Ledge Ruin Overlook and Antelope House Overlook) en route to the Mummy Cave Overlook.

You're almost sure to come across Navajo jewelry vendors on both drives. We found them to be especially friendly here and they offered some of the best prices we saw for native handicrafts and jewelry.

Park Activities

Outdoor activities and attractions are numerous in this area. They include hiking, interpretive exhibits and talks, horseback riding, picnicking, photography and rock art. Many of these require the presence of a guide and you'll need to obtain a permit or special permission for others.

This short but exciting trail provides access to Canyon de Chelly's White House

Four-wheel-drive capability is mandatory for vehicle tours of the canyon. You can rent a vehicle when you arrange for your guide, or you can just hire a guide and drive your own four-wheel-drive vehicle into the canyons.

It's difficult to specify every activity that's allowed or not allowed in this area. The rules are also subject to change from time to time. You're best off contacting the visitor center to inquire about any activities that you're not sure about.

Cottonwood Campground

This is a pretty campground located just inside the park. There are quite a few sites and all the necessary amenities for a good night's rest. You might see the odd stray dog here, but they seem quite friendly.

If you've brought along camping equipment, this is probably your best overnight option. If not, the nearby town of Chinle offers adequate motel accommodations.

Itineraries

1 White House Trail

Distance: 1 mile each way
Time: 30 minutes down; 45 minutes to 1 hr back up
Difficulty: Moderate (elevation gain on the return trip)

This is the only trail in Canyon de Chelly where it's not necessary to have a guide lead you. That also means the trail can get quite busy. Nevertheless, the route is interesting and diverse, and hiking it is a "must".

The only other potential drawback of this route is that the hike back up from the canyon floor can be a hot one, since the trail regains about 500 feet of elevation. Be sure to bring along lots of water and snacks for the kids (and perhaps something for mom and dad, too).

The first part of this trail snakes its way along sandstone slabs high atop a cliff, before looping back around and passing through a cave. The views into the canyon below include glimpses of a working

Navajo farm.

The trail continues to switchback through juniper and pine trees, with natural steps carved into the stone in many places. The descent is gradual but it can be slippery if wet. Along the route, you'll see old sandstone retaining walls, benches and dramatic natural striations in the rock.

The hike flattens out through a sandy wash and then enters a grove of Russian olive and tamarask trees, whose leafy branches spread out like umbrellas overhead. It's a very beautiful path that also provides shade on a hot summer day.

The grove ends at the base of a sheer, red cliff next to a little bridge. Cross the bridge and walk down the dirt road. You may come across Navajo vendors who have spread their goods out on blankets and tables.

Soon you'll reach the ruins, which stretch up from ground level about 50 feet and are tucked into the cliff. Above them rise the massive, red cliffs. Although the ruins are fenced off to prevent visitors getting too close, it's easy to make out the details of each dwelling. Interpretive plaques located nearby will help you understand what you're looking at.

The ruins were named "White House in Between", after the whitewashed walls of the so-called "cultural room" on the upper level of this prehistoric Anasazi village. It's interesting to reflect that this entire area was bustling with life and activity 800 years ago.

Flying high over canyon country

Grand Canyon National Park and Petrified Forest National Park

Hiking to the bottom of the canyon is something that every energetic visitor feels obliged to do.

These two parks — each of which is fantastic in its own right — are quite far from towns that we would consider good "bases" and are therefore best explored on their own. Good accommodation and meals can be found nearby at most times of the year. For families that are prepared to camp out, Grand Canyon National Park offers several nice campsites with all the necessary amenities.

Regardless of how you choose to do it, be sure to explore both parks. Missing the Grand Canyon (one of the great natural wonders of the world) on a trip to the Southwest is simply unforgivable. Bypassing the fascinating science of Petrified Forest National Park would be a travesty, too.

Grand Canyon National Park

The Grand Canyon is not only a World Heritage Site and justifiably famous around the globe, it's also huge! Astronauts have reported that it can be seen by the naked

eye from outer space.

feet lower than some places on the rim — a formidable drop by any standard. It's an even more formidable climb back up, which is why we advise against trying to travel by foot (down and back up) in any fewer than two days.

The Grand Canyon is a fascinating geologic environment and, not surprisingly, is one of the most studied geologic environments in the world. There is no better place to see evidence of land erosion than from its rim and along its edges. A diverse fossil collection, extracted from layers reaching right down to the bottom of the canyon, records the history of ancient organisms over three eras of geologic time.

Paintings and artifacts found in its many caves allude to a more recent (but equally rich) aboriginal past. Some of these items depict organisms that are still found nowhere else but in the Grand Canyon. There are over 1,500 plant, 355 bird, 89 mammal, 47 reptile, nine amphibian and 17 fish species in the park today.

The park itself sprawls over almost 1.3 million acres of the Colorado Plateau country in northwest Arizona. More notable than its size, however, are its climatic extremes. Descending from the rim to the canyon floor is the ecological equivalent of traveling from Canada to Mexico! A thick forest of pine and juniper trees carpets the rim and clings to the upper slopes. Further down, this gives way to increasingly sparse and desert-like vegetation.

The bottom of the canyon, where temperatures are normally 20 degrees Fahrenheit warmer than up top, is as arid as almost any other place in the Southwest. It is also 6,000

To really get a feel for the park's splendor and the fascinating geologic processes that have shaped it over time, try to spend at least two (but preferably three or four) days here. Below are a few suggestions for how to best spend your time while visiting this wonderful place.

Camping

There's no better way to experience the Grand Canyon than by camping beside it. There are several nice campgrounds nearby (as well as a number of backcountry campsites) that will add to an unforgettable experience.

Most campsites are closed during the winter months, except for the South Rim campground. It's located close to the South Rim Visitor Center, which is open year-round. The sites vary in terms of what sort of amenities they offer (and what the overnight fees are), but all provide the basics: tent and RV sites, water and firewood.

Backcountry camping is a great option if you plan to travel to some of the outlying areas, but note that the road to the North Rim is generally closed between mid-October and mid-May. Ask the park staff for a map of backcountry camping sites and check what sort of facilities they provide. (Note that most of them don't have a water supply.)

If camping isn't your thing, the weather's too cold or you haven't brought along camping supplies, consider staying at the South Rim Lodge or at Phantom Canyon Ranch (at the bottom of the Grand Canyon). You'll need to make reservations well in advance if you're planning to visit in the summer — and at several other times of the year, too. To obtain more information, call Xanterra Parks & Resorts at 303-297-2757 or 888-297-2757, or send a fax to 303-297-3175.

Hiking into the Grand Canyon

Hiking to the bottom of the canyon is something that every energetic visitor feels obliged to do. It's an intriguing hike, especially for adults and kids who have a basic appreciation for the geological or climatic regimes they'll pass through en route.

However, the National Park Service wants to impart one very important piece of advice: don't attempt to hike to the bottom of the canyon and back out in just one day — especially with kids! Park personnel will gladly tell anyone who thinks they can pull off this stunt (mainly young and fairly fit 20-year-olds) about the 250 or so rescues they have to arrange every year for those who can't make it back up in time under their own steam.

We suggest two ways to tackle this worthwhile hike. Either only go as far down and back as you and your kids can do comfortably in one day, or else plan to complete the hike as a multi-day trip.

If you choose the first option, we recommend the South Kaibab Trail that descends from the South Rim. It's a narrower and more interesting hike than the Bright Angel Trail, as we found out after hiking that more tedious route. Mule trains don't use the South Kaibab Trail, so there's no need to "share the road" while enjoying the fabulous scenery.

For those who have the time and inclination (and who are fit enough), staying overnight in the canyon at the Phantom Canyon Ranch or in a backcountry campsite is an experience that will be long treasured. Plan ahead for this undertaking by checking out the official National Park Service website at www.nps.gov/grca. Note that reservations for meals and lodging are required for Phantom Canyon Ranch. However, a backcountry permit is not required for overnight stays at its dormitories or cabins. Call 303-297-2757 or 888-297-2757 for additional details.

Beware... It's a long way to the bottom!

The biggest advantage of staying overnight down below — beside the fact that it's the only reasonable way to see the lower canyon environment — is that you'll feel more refreshed (and the air will be relatively cool) when you climb out of the canyon the following morning.

Ride a mule!

Riding a mule down into the Grand Canyon, staying overnight and then riding back up is a good option for those who want to sample this unique experience (or don't feel like making the trip on foot). The tour price covers accommodation, breakfast, lunch and dinner at the Phantom Canyon Ranch (including all taxes) and — of course — the mule ride itself.

If you want to do this, however, you'll have to plan well ahead. Mule trips can be booked as long as 23 months in advance. While planning ahead to this extent may be unnecessary (depend-

unior Ranger Program

The Grand Canyon Junior Ranger Program is a step up from the nature programs offered in many other national parks. Offered mainly in the summer, it's suitable for kids of various ages. They'll either become Ravens (ages four to seven), Coyotes (ages eight to 10) or Scorpions (ages 11 to 14), and can earn the right to wear a kid's version of the official park ranger's badge — which looks just like the real thing.

Kids are asked to complete activities and undertake observations that become increasingly sophisticated as they progress, depending on age and experience. At the highest level, they use binoculars, a hand lens, field guides and other important tools that a real park ranger naturalist would work with.

For more information on the program, drop into a visitor center within Grand Canyon National Park or check out the website at www.nps.grca.

be at least 4 feet 7 inches tall (140 cm), must be in good physical condition, should not be afraid of heights or large animals, and can't be pregnant. For more information about the mules rides offered in the Grand Canyon, contact Xanterra Parks & Resorts by calling (303) 297-2757 or toll free at (888) 297-2757, by fax at (303) 297-3175 or by mail at: Xanterra Parks & Resorts, 14001 E. Illiff, Ste. 600, Aurora, CO 80014.

Petrified Forest National Park

Simply put, Petrified Forest National Park contains one of the world's largest and most colorful collections of petrified wood. The surrounding landscape of "badlands" rock formations, arid grassland and stands of juniper trees has an integral beauty as well, but it's this geologic treasure trove that your family will really want to explore.

The fossils that you'll see are about 225 million years old (dating back to the late Triassic Period) and visiting geologists find new ones every year. Dozens of significant samples are readily accessible and easy to see in several places that are literally just a stroll from the car park.

The park is only open to the public during daylight hours, which will obviously vary depending on the season. (Go online to www.nps.gov/pefo to check the opening hours during the period you want to visit.) Therefore, if you want to stay in the area overnight, you'll have to find accommodations nearby. One day — or even an afternoon — is probably sufficient time to spend there anyway. The following are some short walks we'd recommend:

ing on the time of year you want to visit), it's less likely that you'll be able to take advantage of a last-minute cancellation.

Alternatively, a one-day mule trip is available that only goes partway down the Bright Angel Trail and then returns to the rim, with Plateau Point as the turnaround point. This tour takes about seven hours to complete (down and back up) and includes a box lunch.

Note that mule riders must not weigh more than 200 pounds (91 kg) fully dressed, must

Puerco Pueblo (the trailhead is

Petrified Forest's geology is as colorful as it is fascinating

at Mile Marker 11)

Although this trail is only 0.3 miles long, it has lots to offer. You and the kids can see the ruins of a 100-room pueblo dwelling left behind by the Puebloan people, who lived here between 1,200 and 700 years ago. You'll also see petroglyphs among the remains.

Blue Mesa (the trailhead is at the

Blue Mesa Sun Shelter)

Along this one-mile loop, hikers can get an up-close look at many plant fossils (including delicate ferns) in a badlands landscape of bluish bentonite clay.

Long Logs (the trailhead is at the Rainbow Forest parking area)

Long Logs is home to one of the biggest collections of petrified wood in the park — and therefore in the world. This loop trail's main feature is a fossilized logjam at the base of some gray badlands. The 1.6-mile route brings you back to the parking area. You can pick up a park map (and other information) at the park gates and at the visitor center.

Petrified Forest National Park

is about 3.5 hours by car from Phoenix (214 miles via Payson and Heber) or about three hours from Albuquerque, New Mexico.

Sedona

Red rock formations — from gnarly crags to mystic mountain bluffs — define the landscape.

With its ritzy art galleries, posh resort hotels and New Age "vortex tours", Sedona may not seem like a typical family destination at first. That's absolutely true; **as a base** it's way beyond typical.

Beautiful red rock canyon country surrounds Sedona

Sedona is a wonderful family playground that offers plenty of biking, hiking and water activities. It's a place where you can take an old-fashioned western train ride, go trout fishing and swoosh down a natural rock waterslide — all in the same day. Travel 40 miles to the north of this desert oasis and you'll also experience some of the best skiing in the western United States.

The terrain around Sedona is some of the prettiest in America. Red rock formations — from gnarly crags to mystic mountain bluffs — define the landscape. Huge stands of oak trees are scattered on either side of a creek that winds its way from the mountains in the north to the desert in the south.

That's a lot to recommend a town that was almost named "Schnebly". (Thankfully, the U.S. Postal Service decided

not to name it after the local postmaster, but after his wife instead.)

From the time the Schneblys arrived in the 1900s to the late 1930s, the quiet community was inhabited by farming and ranching families. Things started to change in the 1940s and 1950s when Hollywood came to town. Classic westerns like Billy the Kid and Apache were filmed around Sedona during that period.

The Hollywood connection attracted new residents in the 1960s and 1970s, particularly artists. The Cowboy Artists of America organization was established here in 1965, in an effort to preserve the history of the American West through representative artistic works. For example, a 7.5-foot-tall bronze statue located on Sedona's main street depicts a cowboy painting the nearby red rocks.

By the 1980s, Sedona started attracting large numbers of "New Agers", who claimed to have discovered energy vortexes in areas such as Bell Rock and Boynton Canyon (see below). More recently, outdoor recreation enthusiasts have flocked to the area.

Outdoor pursuits aside, this town of 10,000 people (tucked into Oak Creek Canyon) has much to offer — and it won't necessarily cost you a fortune either. There's a wide range of campgrounds, RV parks and family motels in the surrounding area, as well as a slew of family-friendly eating establishments. Healthy competition between outdoor gear shops means that renting a bike for the day is generally cheaper than in places like Moab.

Following are some suggestions for how best to spend time in the area.

A strange Twist

Some people say that kids are more sensitive to the Earth's inherent "energy" because they haven't yet become so jaded that they dismiss such ideas out of hand. If that's true, then Sedona could provide quite a boost of energy for your entire family.

The area is said to be home to energy "vortexes". Many definitions exist to describe what a vortex actually is, but most agree that it's a point where the Earth's energy is keenly focused: a place of invisible, swirling energy that rejuvenates the body and soul. There are four famous vortexes located around Sedona. Bell Rock and Airport Mesa are thought to contain electric (masculine) energy that will boost your emotional and physical energy levels. Cathedral Rock is considered to be a place of magnetic (feminine) energy, which helps you relax. Boynton Canyon is said to be a place of electromagnetic energy, where visitors can balance both their male and female energies.

Thousands of New Age tourists from around the world flock to Sedona to visit the vortexes every year. If their enthusiasm doesn't convince you, then maybe the harshly twisted juniper trees found near some of the vortexes will.

Activities in the Sedona area:

Slide Rock Park

This park is named after Slide Rock, a famous stretch of slippery creek bottom. Kids and adults alike will have a blast sliding down it. The slick, natural water chute and nearby swimming area have served as backdrops for numerous Hollywood movies.

When you're done cooling off at the slide, there are seven hiking trails and two self-guided interpretive trails in the vicinity to

Oak Creek flows through Slide Park near Sedona

the area are provided along the way. Ask about special rates for children.

To get to the depot, take Highway 89A west to Cottonwood. Head down Main Street through the old part of town (you'll have to leave the highway) until you see a large green sign marked "Train Depot". Drive across the bridge to find the parking lot.

For more information, call 1-800-320-0718.

Rainbow Trout Farm

If you'd like some fresh fish for lunch, this may be your best bet. Located on the banks of Oak Creek Canyon, the farm raises its trout stock in pure artesian springs. Once you've caught lunch, the on-site barbecue grills and picnic tables allow you to easily cook and serve it. No license is required to fish here. To get to the trout farm, drive 3.5 miles (six kilometres) north of Sedona on Highway 89A.

explore. They're all well-marked and family-friendly. Several picnic areas and an apple orchard can also be found nearby. In the fall, be sure to buy a bag of apples.

To get to Slide Rock Park, drive seven miles (11 kilometres) north of Sedona on Highway 89A.

For more information, call 928-282-5799.

Verde Canyon Railway

This four-hour train trip will take you over trestle bridges, through red rock tunnels and alongside meandering desert rivers. Bald eagles, blue herons and coyotes are often seen en route. Music and a live narrative about the history and geography of

Clemeceau Heritage Museum

A far cry from what your kids experience in the classroom, these 19th-century schoolrooms feature old-fashioned inkwells and rustic blackboards. There's also a working model railroad diorama that re-creates the seven railroads that operated in the area between 1895 and 1953, as well as the copper mining towns that they served. The museum is worth a visit, especially if you're planning on riding the Verde Canyon Railway (see above).

For more information, call 928-634-2868.

Snowbowl Ski Area

Located in Flagstaff, Snowbowl is a great year-round destination near Sedona. In the summer, the tramway whisks you to an elevation of more than 11,500 feet, offering views as far afield as the Grand Canyon. There are numerous hiking trails at the top that are suitable for families. In winter, the trails become the prized domain of down-hill skiers, snowboarders and snowshoe enthusiasts.

There are runs that are suitable for kids of all abilities, and lessons and equipment rentals are available on-site. To get to Snowbowl,

drive seven miles northwest of Flagstaff on Highway 180, turn right on Snowbowl Road and then continue on for another seven miles. From Sedona, it will take you about an hour to complete the trip.

For more information, call 928-779-1951.

Flagstaff

Flagstaff is a cool university town of about 50,000 people and (especially in the historic district) is an incredibly livable place. This was one of the most important stopping-off points on historic Route 66, with many buildings and other sites remaining from the famous highway's heyday.

Today, Flagstaff is a great base for lots of outdoor activities. The city's outdoor equipment shops (all of which stock kids' gear) will soon have you outfitted and ready for the trail. Once you've arranged your gear for the day, don't miss out on a good meal

Awesome mountain biking in red rock canyon country

downtown. There's a fantastic Mexican restaurant on the main street called "Martan's" that serves up cheese crisps and great guacamole. Kid's portions are available — and necessary!

Easy and fun biking characterizes the main Bell Rock Trail

Mountain Biking

Sedona (along with Moab and one or two other spots) is one of the best destinations in the Southwest for mountain biking. A combination of great trails, varied topography and beautiful red rock scenery should make you eager to head for the hills, if you're so inclined.

It's beyond the scope of this book to provide an in-depth description of Sedona's many mountain biking opportunities, but we've suggested one easy loop (described below) that almost any kid or parent can handle — or at least those who have spent at least some time biking off-road.

If you're craving more adventure after giving this route a try, ask the locals for

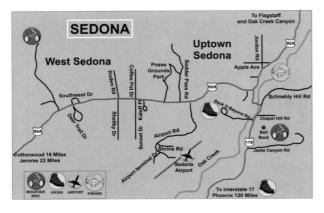

towards Sedona (3.5 miles each way).

These rides begin north of the junction of Highway 179 and Bell Rock Boulevard, just before you enter the village of Oak Creek on the road that runs south from Sedona. There's a convenient parking area located beside the trailhead on the east side of the road.

advice on additional routes. (Bike shops are great resources for up-to-date information.) Alternatively, do some advance research on the Internet or pick up a copy of Mountain Biking Flagstaff and Sedona (Bruce Grubbs, A Falcon Guide) or Arizona Mountain Bike Trail Guide (Cosmic Ray - name of publisher *and* author).

Bell Rock Loops

These fairly short biking loops are located just below Bell Rock and Courthouse Butte, near the village of Oak Creek. They offer lots of fun riding with very little need for technical ability and/or ability to do a long ride, and are easily accessible. If you'd rather bike along a wider path with a specific destination in mind, simply stay on the main Bell Rock pathway as it winds north

The trail starts out as a wide, sandy track. Even though it's a little soft at the beginning, the going gets easier quite quickly. The first Bell Rock loop begins at the second (and marked) right-hand turn on this path, on a considerably narrower trail. It heads northeast for about 1.5 miles, passing through a pretty landscape filled with juniper, red rock and sandy washes.

The trail abruptly curves back in the direction you came from and after 0.4 miles offers a couple of options for the return trip. Both are nice routes, but the right-hand one is a little longer.

Once you return to the Bell Rock pathway, either turn left (south) to reach the parking lot or head north to discover other excellent trails.

Sedona, Arizona

Travel times to:

Flagstaff: via Highway 89 (north); 45 minutes
Phoenix: via Highway 179 (south), Highway 17 (south); 2 hours
Las Vegas: via Highway 89 (north), Highway 40 (west), Highway 93 (north); 5 hours
Grand Canyon: via Highway 89 (north), Highway 40 (west), Highway 64 (north); 2 hours
Tucson: via Highway 179 (south), Highway 17 (south); 2 hours. Highway 10 (south); 4 hours

Organ Pipe Cactus National Monument

This is a real desert wilderness of the sort you and your kids may have dreamt about.

Few tourists make it as far south as Organ Pipe Cactus National Monument, and perhaps that's part of its charm. This is a real desert wilderness of the sort you and your kids may have dreamt about, with umpteen varieties of cactus — including the giant saguaro and, of course, the majestic organ pipe — and lots of desert critters to go with them.

Here, more than in most other parts of the Southwest, you can drive along deserted roads, hike quiet trails, camp under brilliant, starry skies and just relax in the warmth and wonder of the desert landscape.

This part of the Sonoran Desert is big (about 330,000 acres) and is almost completely unspoiled by human encroachment. Its wilderness aspect is so significant that the United Nations designated all of Organ Pipe Cactus National Monument an International Biosphere Reserve in 1976.

There's wild and varied topography in Organ Pipe

Remarkable erosion patterns can be found in Organ Pipe Cactus National Monument

Try to make it here if your travel plans can accommodate the trip.

520-387-6849 or check out the website at www.nps.gov/orpi.

Desert View Nature Trail

This 1.2-mile (round trip) circuit is a good introduction to the flora and fauna of Organ Pipe Cactus National Monument. Walking up a wash and then along a ridgeline opens up a 180º panoramic view. Beyond the towering cacti are the surrounding Cubabi Mountains of Mexico, in all their rose-colored glory.

Interpretive signs are posted along the route to help familiarize you with the area. The trail starts at the Organ Pipe campground, 1.5 miles south of the visitor center.

For more information, call

Victoria Mine Trail

The Victoria Mine Trail is a longer hike (4.5 miles) that leads to what was once Organ Pipe Cactus National Monument's

Beautiful cactus blossoms are commonplace along Organ Pipe's trails in the spring

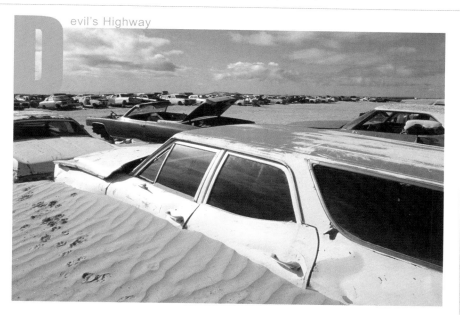

Devil's Highway

Running through the Cabeza Prieta National Wildlife Refuge is the infamous "El Camino del Diablo" (or "Devil's Highway"). The 130-mile route that runs from Sonoyta, Mexico to what is now Yuma, Arizona has claimed the lives of hundreds (perhaps thousands) of people who underestimated its tough traveling conditions.

The road routinely experiences temperatures of 120° F. With water sources few and far between, the route has become one big graveyard.

Jesuit Padre Eusebio Francisco Kino first charted the trail from 1699-1701. His records show that it could be 50 miles between places where potable water could be found. In the 1800s, the California Gold Rush inspired thousands of Mexicans (who were hoping to strike it rich) to travel the route. Many of them were well-equipped with picks and tools to go prospecting, but some of them were hopelessly under-equipped when it came to water supplies.

So why did people keep traveling along this deadly road and not find some other route? In the 1700s, it was simply the quickest way to get from Mexico to the Spanish possession of California, since the road was 150 miles shorter than the route that passed through Tucson. You were also less likely to be attacked by the Apache Indians, who stayed away from the Devil's Highway during the hottest months.

The Apaches were clearly onto something. At the height of summer, it's necessary to drink two gallons of water per day just to survive here. Today, officials responsible for the Cabeza Prieta National Wildlife Refuge warn people not to travel on this dirt road during the summer.

richest gold and silver mine. As well as highlighting a site with great historical value, this hike passes through a beautiful, rolling landscape at the base of the Sonoyta Mountains.

The well-marked route begins at the south end of the Campground Loop Trail and then heads west.

Camping (and goofing around) near Ajo

them with an official junior ranger badge.

Cabeza Prieta National Wildlife Refuge

Directly translated, "cabeza prieta" means "dark head" and the name refers to a black, lava-covered peak in a distant corner of the region. Cabeza Prieta National Wildlife Refuge is the third largest wildlife refuge in the lower 48 states. Created in 1939 to protect the region's population of bighorn sheep, it's home to almost 300 other kinds of animals and 400 species of plants.

Junior Park Ranger Program

Organ Pipe encourages the development of junior park rangers in the same way that most other national park and national monument facilities do. Your kids can start their quest to become junior park rangers by dropping into the visitor center and picking up a workbook. Once all the activities are finished, a ranger will ask them a few questions and then — if all goes well — award

You can drive through the refuge by arranging a permit at the small visitor center, which will also give your kids a better understanding of what a national wildlife refuge is. The exhibits here feature bighorn sheep, the endangered Sonoran pronghorn antelope and other wildlife.

A selection of videos and a short interpretive trail outside the building add to the learning experience. The visitor center is located on the west side of Highway 85, at the north end of town.

This drive should not be attempted without

a four-wheel-drive vehicle, since the roads in the refuge are all covered with loose sand.

For more information, call 520-387-6483 or check the website at www.southwest.fws.gov.

Ajo
as a
base

This quaint little town of 3,000 people has a strong Spanish influence. At the heart of Ajo is a red-tiled plaza, a park, shops and a couple of old, mission-style churches — just like you'd see in any number of Mexican communities.

Mexico is not far away, with the border town of Sonoyta just 30 miles to the south. If you travel another 70 miles south along the same road, you could soon be hitting the beach with your family on the Gulf of California, at Puerto Penasco (see below).

Being so close to Mexico is not the only benefit of Ajo's location. Phoenix is just a two-hour drive north and Tucson is only 2 ½ hours away to the east. Closest of all is Organ Pipe Cactus National Monument, which is just a 30-minute drive away.

The town itself is known as the birthplace of Arizona's copper mining industry. From the 1920s to the 1980s, Ajo was bustling with the sounds of heavy machinery. Since the mine closed in 1984, the town has tried to reinvent itself as a retirement community. Several RV parks around town are testaments to this endeavor.

Though Ajo is a little on the scruffy side in some places, there's a decent selection of motels and restaurants along 2nd Avenue, by the plaza. There's also lots of free camping south of town.

Two supermarkets allow you to stock up on groceries. Unfortunately, despite the town's name, we didn't find any special deals while purchasing "ajo" (garlic).

Activities in the Ajo area:

A Glimpse at Ajo's Past (and Future?)

On the outskirts of Ajo is the New Cornelia Mine. At 1.5 miles in diameter, it's one of the largest open pit mines in the world. Current speculation has it that when copper prices rise high enough, the mine will be reopened. Near the overlook at the mine is a small visitor center with exhibits and videos about the copper industry.

Kids might find the artifacts at the Ajo Historical Society Museum more interesting. There, they'll see exhibits that include a full-scale blacksmith shop, an old dentist's office and a print shop. To get to the mine overlook, follow the signs along Indian Village Road. The museum is at the very end of the road.

For more information, call 520-387-7105 or check the website at www.ajoinaz.com/historical.htm.

Hitting the Beach in Puerto Penasco

After the heat of the desert, your family might welcome a quick jaunt down to the Mexican fishing village of Puerto Penasco ("gringos" call it Rocky Point) at the north-

Puerto Penasco offers a perfect beach reprieve from the surrounding desert

ern end of the Gulf of California.

This has been one of our family's favorite spots since 1991, when we had the fortune (not misfortune) of having our old camper "Jethro" break down. We were therefore "forced" to do some beach camping for a few days. Among other things, we discovered seafood markets galore, which offer fresh shrimp (the shrimp season runs from September to April), oysters, clams and even some octopus. They were the perfect ingredients (or so we learned) for a little homemade ceviche!

If you're driving by car, there are plenty of cheap places to pitch a tent here. A spot at Sandy Beach costs just a few dollars per day. Alternatively, check out some of the beaches south of Rocky Point.

If you're in an RV, there are numerous places that offer showers and full-hook ups. A camping spot will cost $12 to $25 per night, depending on how close you are to the beach.

As befits a beach setting, there's a ton of things for kids to see and do. Dolphins and sea lions abound in this part of the Gulf of California. Hunting for clams, a visit to the local aquarium, and banana boat rides are all fun options as well.

Puerto Penasco is only a two-hour drive from Ajo (94 miles). To get to the beach, follow Highway 85 south from Ajo until you reach the Mexican border. On the other side is the Mexican town of Sonoyta. Stay to the right and watch for signs directing you to Puerto Penasco. You can take Route 8 (a better road than Highway 85) all the way there.

Puerto Penasco lies within a Mexican free trade zone, so the border crossing, visas, shopping and car insurance are all easily managed if you're planning a stay of less than 72 hours. The local newspaper's website (www.rptimes.com) is an excellent resource to help you plan your trip.

There's one thing to watch for, however. Avoid a mid-March trip to Puerto Penasco, unless you want your kids to share their sandcastle space with American college students celebrating spring break.

Ajo

Travel times to:

Phoenix: via Highway 85 (north), Highway 10 (east); 2 hours
Tucson: via Highway 85 (south), Highway 86 (east); 2½ hours
Puerto Penasco: via Highway 85 (south), Highway 8 (south); 2 hours
Organ Pipe Cactus National Monument: via Highway 85 (south); 30 minutes
Sedona: via Highway 85 (north), Highway 17 (north), Highway 179 (north); 3½ hours

ARIZONA

Kayenta

Grand Canyon National Park

Canyon De Chelly National Monument

Lake Mead National Park

Wupatki National Park

Williams

Petrified Forest National Park

Kingman

Flagstaff

Lake Havasu City

Sedona

Show Low

Wickenburg

Alpine

Phoenix

Globe

Gila Bend

Casa Grande

Yuma

Ajo

Saguaro National Park

Organ Pipe Cactus National Monument

Tucson

Wilcox

Green Valley

Tombstone

Puerto Penasco

Sierra Vista

MOUNTAIN BIKE   HIKING   RAFTING

Tucson

Old Tucson will make you feel like you've just stepped onto an Old West movie set.

Unlike other bases suggested in this book, Tucson is a fairly large city. The metropolitan area is home to 900,000 people and it has its share of big city amenities but also a few big city problems. Whether you're comfortable with urban life or reluctant to bring the kids to a large city, the fact remains that Tucson is a particularly good starting point to travel to some of the Southwest's main attractions. If you stay close to Tucson Mountain Park — and we suggest you do — it's possible to sample the best this city has to offer while remaining nicely insulated from its downside.

The main desert parks here are Saguaro National Park and Tucson Mountain Park. They're as pristine as any other in the Southwest, even if more visitors (and the occasional drone of city noise) might slightly interfere with your family's appreciation of the desert solitude.

Little Porkers

If you're hiking with your family in the canyon areas south of Tucson, keep an eye out for other families in the vicinity: Javelinas (by Julia) javelina families. The javelina — pronounce the "j" as an English "h" — is the only wild pig species in North America and its range stretches from the Southwest desert lands all the way to Argentina.

It's a good thing the hairy little critters are found in such abundance, since they're also a very popular target for hunters.

If your kids want to get a good look at these critters, they should search for a two-foot-high and three to four-foot-long animal with coarse, gray fur and short, sharp tusks. Keep an eye out in canyon areas that are shady and contain waterholes, especially if the javelina's favorite foods (the prickly pear and agave cactus) are nearby.

Javelinas like company and can be found in herds of up to 50 animals, which is helpful when it comes to protecting themselves from predators like humans and coyotes. Since javelinas blend in with the washed-out colors of the desert environment, they're sometimes hard to spot and can often be heard or smelled long before they're seen. They make sounds ranging from snorts and squeals to loud barks, and they emit a strong odor thanks to the musk gland on their rumps.

Tucson International Airport is low-key and especially well-suited for accessing the parkland located on the city's western edge. Flying in, renting a car and driving to a trailhead situated amongst stands of saguaro cactus is easy and fast — incredibly so.

We highlight a few of the Tucson area's finest natural treasures and cultural experiences in the following section, without really touching on any of its impressive urban amenities. If you'd like to know more about the city itself, log onto www.visittucson.org or www.ci.tucson.az.us.

Tucson Mountain Park

Tucson Mountain Park, in combination with Saguaro National Park immediately to the northwest, justifies at least one overnight stay in Tucson. One nice attraction for kids within the park is Old Tucson, which has the feel of a movie set but the amenities of an amusement park (see below).

But the park's natural history and the adventure opportunities it offers are the real stars. If you spend enough time here, you can expect to see roadrunners, javelinas, coyotes, rabbits and even rattlesnakes. Hiking and biking are popular activities (see below) and you can also hire horses for trail rides.

If you do nothing else, make sure that you allow at least an hour or two to drive through the park, allowing enough time for a few stops along the way. Your kids will love the southernmost part of the route (Kinney Road) for its series of dips that make it feel — even when driven at a

Even driving is a thrill in Tucson Mountain Park

moderate speed — like they're on a roller-coaster.

David Vetnam Trail

With its trailhead only 15 minutes from downtown Tucson, this is as accessible a hike as you could ever hope for. It's also a beautiful one and provides an in-depth look at flora and fauna that you'd only expect of a true "wilderness" hike.

The David Vetnam Trail makes a nice "through" hike with kids, if you have two vehicles with you or if someone is willing to drop off the rest of the group up top and then park down below. Otherwise, we suggest hiking to the highest point of land and turning around there.

The trail description that follows is from east to west. Just reverse the order of the directions if you start from Tucson Mountain Park. We'd recommend the latter approach

if you're hiking with kids, since most of the route will then be downhill. Try to get an early morning start, because the short uphill section will still be in the shade.

You can ride most of this trail on mountain bikes, although probably only if your kids are fit and experienced. You may want to confirm with the park staff that the trail is currently open to bikes before renting any gear. The best advice we can give you is to ride (and push) your bike up to the high point of land from the west parking lot. That way, much of the route will be a bumpy, downhill coast.

To get to the trail, drive west from Tucson's city center along Speedway Boulevard to reach Camino del Oeste, in the hilly residential area of West Tucson (just before you reach the International Wildlife Museum). Turn left (south) and follow this road past the point where the pavement stops and the gravel begins, and continue to the very end. You'll see a small parking area on your right. If it's full, be careful not to block the access to any of the private homes when you eventually find a parking spot.

The trail immediately crosses a wash and then rises gently through a narrow valley studded with at least five different varieties of cacti. Note how the majestic saguaro cactus is more prevalent on the south side than the north side. This is because the cactus can't survive on the shadier north slopes during the Tucson winter's relatively cold temperatures.

Great hiking — or challenging mountain biking — along the David Vetnam Trail

Continue climbing for about an hour until you come to the highest point of land and an intersection with a trail that leads to Gates Pass. The westernmost car park is only 15 minutes ahead of you. If you didn't arrange for a car to pick you up there, this

is probably the best place to turn around — once you've enjoyed the great vistas.

Old Tucson

Old Tucson will make you feel like you've just stepped onto an Old West movie. In fact, Old Tucson was named "Best Western Movie Set" in 2005 by the readers and editors of True West magazine. As a filming location for hundreds of movies since 1939, Old Tucson hosts film and television productions throughout the year and also offers "daily Wild West entertainment for the whole family!"

Your kids will almost certainly be spellbound by the regularly scheduled "gunfights", as well as the comic performances and musical revues. This is the kind of place that even parents who have been hardened by too many trips to amusement parks will appreciate. The beautiful setting certainly helps.

Your family can head down Memory Lane on the park's well-designed daily tours (or on the miniature train), get dressed up in old-fashioned duds for a photograph, or

Details of Old Tucson

Old Tucson is a moviemaker's paradise

within Tucson Mountain Park (it's located less than a mile east of the park boundary), you and your kids are sure to enjoy it. Billed as "Tucson's Natural History Museum", the International Wildlife Museum showcases over 400 species of insects, birds and mammals from around the world.

All of the museum's animals have been donated by government organizations, zoos and wildlife rehabilitation centers. Dioramas, videos, computer programs and hands-on exhibits provide kids and adults alike with an interactive wildlife experience and a more thorough understanding of conservation issues. The Safari Club International Foundation, a non-profit environmental organization, runs the museum.

For more information, check the website at www.thewildlifemuseum.org or phone 520-629-0100.

enjoy some fine western fare at lunch or dinner. Be sure to check out "The Reno" locomotive on your visit; this vintage, immaculately maintained piece of history already has over 100 television and film credits on its resumé.

Find out more about Old Tucson by visiting www.oldtucson.com or by phoning 520-883-0100.

International Wildlife Museum

Although this museum is not technically

Saguaro National Park

Named after the most recognizable cactus in the world, Saguaro National Park is a treasure trove of unique desert scenery. Just driving through the park is a thrilling experience, but spending a little more time on the ground (hiking some of its 150 miles of trails, for example) is even more rewarding.

Saguaro cacti are not only the namesake sentinels of this desert environment. They also produce sweet fruit that several species of animals feed on and they provide homes for birds such as the Harris' hawk, the Gila woodpecker and the elf owl. In turn, the saguaro relies on other desert plants such as the palo verde tree for its own survival.

Saguaros can reach a height of 50 feet and live an average of 150 years. The park staff will be happy to tell you more about them and this beautiful desert region, or point you toward hiking trails that are most appropriate for your family.

Another portion of Saguaro National Park lies just east of Tucson and consists of the same kind of terrain. You can continue your exploration of this fascinating desert environment with a visit to that section of the park. Go online to www.nps. gov/sagu/ to find out more.

The beautiful saguaros of Saguaro National Park are just a long stone's throw from the city limits

del Bac is easy to visit en route to or from Tucson International Airport. It's located just a few miles away to the southwest. Known affectionately as "The White Dove of the Desert", this mission is still very active and has a history as rich as its exterior architecture and interior artwork.

The surrounding area was known as "the Bac" by the Tohono O'odham natives, and the name means "place where water appears". The site was visited by the famous Jesuit missionary and explorer Father Eusebio Francisco Kino in 1692. He established a church roughly two miles north of the present mission and named it after an illustrious Jesuit figure, St. Francis Xavier.

Others followed in Kino's footsteps and the mission (as it now stands) was built between 1783 and 1797. Curiously, one tower was not completed during this construction phase and the omission remains an unsolved mystery to this day.

San Xavier's beautiful paintings (and other artwork) were created in the years that followed the mission's construction. They and the exterior walls have deteriorated somewhat after hundreds of years' worth of harsh desert sun and wind. Most of the artwork, however, remains beautifully intact and some pieces are now being delicately

Junior Ranger Program

Like other national parks, this one offers Junior Ranger programs as well as Junior Ranger Camps in the summer. For more information, check out the website at www. nps.gov/sagu/ and click on "Kids".

San Xavier Del Bac Mission

Arguably the most beautiful of the Southwest's mission buildings, San Xavier

restored.

We strongly suggest that you visit this stunning monument to human exploration of the Southwest — possibly the most extraordinary example of mission architecture anywhere in the U.S. Franciscan Friars conduct regular services within its walls and the mission is open to the public during daytime hours. Admission is free, but donations are welcomed.

The easiest way to get to the mission is to turn west off Highway 19 onto West San Xavier Road, about nine miles south of downtown Tucson. After less than a mile on this road, a sign will direct you north to the mission entrance. Alternatively, approach it from South Mission Road, turning east where the directional signs indicate.

One of the most captivating examples of mission architecture to be found anywhere

Tombstone

Any kid with a penchant for western movies will already have Tombstone (and its infamous OK Corral) firmly embedded in his or her psyche. It's hard for parents to resist this place, too, especially once they learn it's located nearby.

As one of the most illustrious sites in Wild West folklore, Tombstone has more recently become known as "The Town Too Tough to Die". It got its original name when a

Downtown Tombstone today, and pretty much as it's always been

soldier named Ed Schieffelin was told that he'd find his tombstone, rather than riches, when he left his company to stake a claim and seek a fortune in silver. He discovered a bonanza in 1877, as did the others who arrived to prospect that year. The next few years of the town's history were characterized by lawlessness and violence, and military troops were almost dispatched to restore order. The tension culminated in the famous Wyatt Earp-Clanton gunfight, which occurred in the OK Corral on Oct. 26, 1881.

For the next seven years, Tombstone's mines produced millions of dollars worth of silver and gold. Rising underground water then forced the miners to quit. The town's glorious mining days weren't completely finished, though. Tombstone became a leading producer of manganese during the First World War and of lead during the Second World War.

Rather than let Tombstone fade into obscurity, its citizens determinedly pinned their hopes for the town's future on historical restoration and tourism. In that endeavor, they've been very successful. Several of Tombstone's buildings are fine examples of 1880s American craftsmanship. The best among them are St. Paul's Episcopal Church (built in 1882), the Crystal Palace Saloon (once one of the most luxurious saloons in the West) and the Tombstone Epitaph building (where newspapers are still being printed).

Visitors to Tombstone will be thrilled by its well-preserved history. Souvenirs, snack foods and even the sidewalks will make your kids feel as though they've stepped back in time to a place they've only fantasized about or seen in movies. Regularly scheduled "gunfights" at the OK Corral make it seem even more real to active imag-

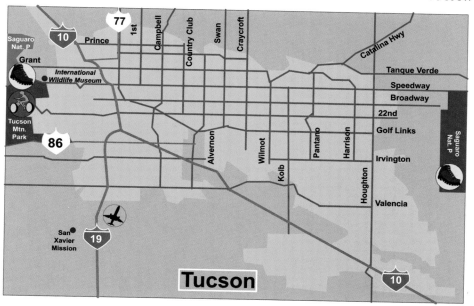

inations. We highly recommend taking in the experience.

You can get to Tombstone from Tucson by driving east on Highway 10 for about 35 miles to Benson, and then south on Highway 80 for another 24 miles. The trip takes about an hour.

For more information, check the website at www.cityoftombstone.com or phone 800-457-3423.

New Mexico and Western Texas

Whitesands National Monument has simply the most beautiful natural sand dunes we've ever seen.

New Mexico's charms are equal parts natural and manmade

The eastern fringe of the Southwest is — for our family, at least — defined by New Mexico and a little bit of western Texas. Other people might include more of the Lone Star State, but our preference is to corral things a little bit tighter. We hope you don't mind…

New Mexico is an integral part of the Southwest experience and offers much that is unique. The city of Santa Fe is just one example. There is no other place in the Southwest (or perhaps in the entire United States) that manages to create such a perfect blend of "boutique" culture and historical culture. White Sands National Monument contains the most beautiful natural sand dunes we've ever seen and some of the caves in Carlsbad Caverns National Park are the largest of their kind in the Western Hemisphere.

It's a long way from California to New Mexico, especially for kids cooped up in the back of a car. We wouldn't recommend

that people drive the entire route between them unless they've set aside lots of time to explore, they have a very comfortable motorhome or they're willing to catch an occasional flight to take a break from life on the road.

New Mexico is an especially easy state to explore. Roads are generally in good shape and free of heavy traffic, and the distances between points of interest aren't any more onerous than elsewhere in the Southwest. So go ahead and explore this magical land of pueblo architecture and natural beauty! You won't be disappointed that you made the extra effort and neither will your kids.

Santa Fe

In many ways, Santa Fe is the heart and soul of the entire Southwest. It's a beautiful city and cultural smorgasbord all rolled into one, and an absolute "must see" destination for families traveling to the areas covered in this guide.

Santa Fe was founded in 1610 and is the oldest capital city in North America. It's therefore an incredibly historic place. It is home to the United States' oldest church, its oldest inhabited house and its oldest public building. It also hosts the nation's oldest annual community celebration (the Santa Fe Fiesta), which was first held in 1712.

Scenes of Santa Fe beg to be explored.

Santa Fe's San Miguel church is the oldest of its kind in North America

The Santa Fe art scene is legendary. More art is created and sold here than anywhere else in the U.S., with the possible exception of New York City. Native art is represented particularly well and its influence even flows into much of the non-Native work on display here.

Even if your kids don't normally enjoy visiting museums or gazing at works of art, a trip to one of Santa Fe's fabled cultural institutions (the Museum of Fine Arts or the Indian Arts Museum, for example) will surely raise their eyebrows. It might also prompt intriguing questions such as: "Was great-granddad born yet when…?" or "Why did they build their homes like that?"

To put things into proper perspective, the city of Santa Fe was established 10 years before the Pilgrims landed in America aboard the Mayflower in 1620. Michelangelo finished painting the ceiling of the Sistine Chapel less than a century earlier and an English fellow by the name of William Shakespeare was still writing plays.

Santa Fe was once the site of several Pueblo Indian villages. The Spanish capital of "The Kingdom of New Mexico" was originally

It didn't survive long as a Mexican possession, however. In the early days of the Mexican-American War (1846-1848), Santa Fe was captured for the U.S. by General Philip Kearny. American traders and trappers, who had often been seen around town previously, arrived in increasing numbers. Santa Fe prospered and grew even wealthier with the arrival of the railroad and the telegraph decades later.

established 25 miles north of the city's present location, but the capital was moved south in 1610.

Over the next 80 years, Spanish soldiers and Franciscan missionaries tried to subdue the area's Pueblo Indians and convert them to Christianity. The Indians eventually revolted, killing at least 400 Spaniards and driving the rest back into Mexico. They also razed almost every Spanish building in the city, except for the Palace of the Governors.

Spain's Don Diego de Vargas reconquered Santa Fe and the surrounding region in 1692, ushering in a period of relative calm and prosperity under the Spaniards that lasted until 1821. In that year, Mexico gained its independence from Spain and Santa Fe became the capital of the province of New Mexico.

Corruption in government became the bedfellow of prosperity, however. Things eventually got so bad that U.S. President Rutherford Hayes appointed Lew Wallace (a stern figure indeed) to clean up the town. He did the job with such fervor and success that the outlaw Billy the Kid threatened Wallace with certain death if he were to continue cleaning corruption up. Unfazed, Wallace carried on his crime-fighting ways.

Santa Fe's fine museums were created during the early part of the 20th century, as locals and visitors came to appreciate the city's historic significance. This was followed in 1958 by the passing of a strict code that mandated a distinctly Spanish-Pueblo architectural style, based on adobe (mud and straw) and wood construction.

Modern visitors are the beneficiaries of these developments, which can be attributed to the foresight of past citizens and government officials. Whatever else you do in town, be sure to walk through the streets that surround the Plaza, check out the San Miguel Mission (and the nearby historic buildings) and have a look at Santa Fe's unique state capitol building.

A day or two is long enough to see most of the local sights, but you could easily spend a few days just walking through the historic districts. Here are a few other activities to try, if you have more time to explore the surrounding area.

Activities in the New Mexico and Western Texas area:

Taos

Taos truly is "an Indian Pueblo, a Spanish village, a world-class ski resort, a historic art colony...[and] a state of mind", as its official website boasts. The Taos area enjoys 300 days of sunshine and 300 inches of snowfall every year,
all of which creates endless opportunities for adventure and discovery.

Mountain biking, rock climbing, hiking

and rafting are well-developed summer activities. Hot air ballooning over the Rio Grande Gorge comes with a unique "splash and dash" feature.

Winter sports have made the Taos area famous world over. Skiing – both downhill and cross-country - snowshoeing, snowmobiling and ice fishing are often excellent from late December through late March. Four resorts in the Taos area cater to downhill skiers of all ability levels, offering easy cruising runs, moderate terrain and lots of black diamonds. Taos claims the best of "champagne powder" - the arid climate and high altitude literally suck water out of falling snow.

Its topography is as exciting as the skiing. The tallest mountains in New Mexico frame Taos' northeastern horizon; southwest of town high desert mesas and the deep Rio Grande Gorge define the landscape.

To get to Taos from Santa Fe, take Hwy 285 to Hwy 68. It is about 75 miles away, and is about a 1¼ hour drive.

For more info, visit www.taosguide.com

Albuquerque Balloon festival

The Albuquerque Balloon Festival is the

largest such event in the world. From its humble beginnings in 1972, when 13 balloons sailed aloft, it now sees nearly 800 balloons take to the skies each year with over 1,000 pilots involved.

This festival is held during the first week of October and includes mass ascensions on the weekends and some very quirky balloons. Even if you're not a fan of hot air ballooning, you'll find this is an incredibly colorful event (in terms of both balloons and people).

For more information, check the website at www.aibf.org.

For more info, visit www.aibf.org

White Sands National Monument

What kid (or adult, for that matter) can resist acres of squeaky clean Caribbean-like sand arranged in perfect dune formations? White Sands National Monument is a playground of the very best sort.

Just like in California's Death Valley, many dunes here have one or more steep sides. These beg to have kids somersault down or catapult across them. The crests are fabulous places to throw a Frisbee or just admire your footprints in the sand.

Is it snow? Nope, it's sand.

This is an incredibly beautiful place and it's been used as a location for hundreds of fashion and product photography shoots over the years, involving some of the finest photographers in the business. If you've driven a long way to get here, you'll probably just want to sit back and soak in the beauty of the place (or perhaps after exercising your road-weary body a bit).

White Sands National Monument is home to a diverse and unique range of desert flora and fauna. Several animals have adapted to their dazzling environment with camouflage that is as white as the gypsum sand itself. The aptly named bleached earless lizard is one of these interesting critters.

Hiking through White Sands' fabulous dune country

Although it's rather ominous (but kind of cool at the same time, at least for some kids), White Sands National Monument is entirely surrounded by the White Sands Missile Range. The visitor center showcases several of the first missiles that flew across this area. In fact, they're among the first missiles that flew anywhere. On a sour note, White Sands National Monument and a portion of Highway 70 are closed to traffic whenever tests are being conducted. The closures last an average of one to two hours, twice a week.

Park rangers offer nature walks, evening slide programs and star talks, at least during the summer. Kids are welcome to take part in these.

White Sands National Monument may seem like it's out in the back of beyond, but it's not too far away if you happen to be passing through El Paso, Texas or Las Cruces, New Mexico. Probably the best way to include it in your itinerary is to stop here while taking our suggested driving route through the eastern Desertlands. (See the "Suggested Driving Circuits" section in the Southwest Highways chapter.)

Once you arrive at the historic adobe visitor center just off of Highway 70 (15 miles west of Alamogordo), you're only minutes away from playing in the dunes. A nominal fee gives you access to the dunes until the evening closing time, which varies according to the time of year. The road takes you right into the heart of the dunes after about eight miles. We suggest going all the way to the end of the road before parking, however, since you can always sample some of the short hikes along the roadside on your way back.

Although the park has no official campground, backcountry camping is sometimes permitted at specific sites (inquire at visitor center), and three campgrounds are located within 35 miles of its boundaries. Motel accommodation is quite plentiful in nearby Alamogordo, as are restaurants and many other tourist facilities.

Carlsbad Caverns National Park

Simply put, the Carlsbad Caverns are fantastic. They may not be the largest, longest or most beautiful caverns on the planet, but most cave aficionados rank them on their personal "Top 10" list of favorite caves.

Carlsbad Caverns National Park was founded in 1930 (after being named a national monument just five years earlier) to protect the main cavern complex and over 100 other caves nearby. In 1995, it was named a World Heritage Site. The park is nearly 50,000 acres in size, about two-thirds of which is a designated wilderness area.

Even the road leading into the park is pretty. Leaving Highway 62 about 20 miles west of the town of Carlsbad, New Mexico, it winds through a limestone canyon for seven miles before cresting on top of the plateau where the visitor center and parking area are located. (On the way back, consider taking the one-way scenic loop along the plateau crest and then down through Walnut Canyon. It will only add about 10 miles to the drive.)

After buying your cavern exploration ticket at the visitor center, you have a choice of speeding down to the main cavern by elevator or hiking down from the "natural" entrance and through the bat caves. The elevator ride takes 58 seconds, while the walk takes about one hour. Both routes descend about 750 feet to arrive at the same spot.

Located at this depth — unbelievably — is a snack bar and gift shop. Park personnel will tell you that you're not allowed to eat or drink beyond this point. You also can't "touch, litter, spit, smoke or chew gum" while touring the caves. In addition, you'll be asked to keep a lid on loud noise in an effort to preserve the tranquility of the place. (Note that strollers are not allowed in the caves, due to the steep and narrow trails.)

Self-guided exploration is allowed along a one-mile loop that passes through the Big Room, while a park ranger will accompany you through other parts of the cave, such as the King's Palace. This 1½-hour tour will not fail to impress any member of your group. The paved path was skillfully constructed to wind through intriguing clusters of stalactites, alongside dripwater pools and above deep chasms. The lighting fixtures have been expertly arranged to draw your attention to the cave's main features along the way.

Audio guides are available at the visitor center for anyone who wants a more thorough introduction to the caves, although they're not absolutely necessity. Interpretive plaques have been installed all along the route and spell out much of the same information that's included in the audio tour. Points of interest are identified with

Driving to Carlsbad's visitor center, where it's always warm inside!

Exploring the Big Room

The Bat Cave

Batman would be proud.

Carlsbad Caverns National Park is home to an estimated 300,000 of the superhero's flying friends, from the Big Brown Bat to the Western Small-footed Myotis. Although that number may seem very high, it's only a third of what was thought to exist in 1898, when a cowboy named James White first entered the cavern. Legend has it that White thought he saw a plume of smoke emanating from the cavern entrance, but it turned out to be a massive column of bats on the wing.

The ancestors of those bats take to the air each night during the summer for their evening flight, which has turned into a major tourist attraction. The bats, mostly females, roost on the ceiling of the cave about a half mile inside. When airborne, they are impressive physical specimens and some of them have 11-inch wingspans, despite weighing less than an ounce each.

Most of the creatures here are Mexican free-tailed bats and are easily distinguished by their gray or brown coloring, long and narrow wings, and a skinny, dangling tail. In the autumn, most of the colony migrates south to Mexico, although no one is certain exactly where. They're elusive, just like the Caped Crusader himself.

With the bat population dwindling at Carlsbad Caverns National Park, the visitor center has started up an Adopt-a-Bat program. Its goal is to stop the loss of natural bat habitat that has taken place over the past century. Have you ever thought about putting a bat house in your backyard? This is where you can learn how to do it.

discreet signs. (See if your kids can spot the Mirror Lake sign, which is cleverly illegible — except when seen on the surface of the lake itself.)

Carlsbad Caverns National Park is a great place to visit on any day that you find too hot, too cold or otherwise inclement, since the temperature inside the cave remains a steady 56º F year-round. The caves are open every day of the year except Christmas Day.

Open rangelands in Guadalupe Mountains National Park

Guadalupe Mountains National Park (Texas)

Much of Highway 62, which runs east of Hueco Tanks (see below), is flat as a pancake — or at least until you arrive at Guadalupe Mountains National Park. Once a stop for Butterfield stagecoaches travelling between San Francisco and St. Louis, this dramatic mass of mountains is part of one of the world's largest Permian Era fossil reefs.

Although most of the limestone rock is too crumbly to climb on, Guadalupe Mountains National Park has 80 miles of hiking trails and a couple of worthwhile backpacking trips that lead through beautiful, high desert terrain. Camping (at either the Pine Springs campsite or the Dog Canyon campsite) is a great way to experience the park. So is four-wheel-driving along its gravel roads. Inquire about these and other activities at the park's visitor center, located just off of Highway 62.

The ruins of the original stagecoach station are worth checking out, as are some of the park's numerous petroglyphs and the Frijole Ranch Museum. We'd advise you to combine a stop here with a visit to Carlsbad

Make advance reservations to visit the park if at all possible, since park staff restrict the number of visitors that are allowed into the park at any one time. Especially on weekends and holidays, visitors without reservations may be turned away. Call 512-389-8900 to make a reservation over the phone and the cost will be deducted from your entrance fee when you arrive.

Boulders beg to be climbed at Hueco Tanks, one of North America's best places for the sport

Caverns National Park and Hueco Tanks State Historical Park, or include it in a broader circuit route. (See the "Suggested Driving Circuits" in the Southwest Highways chapter.)

For more information, phone 915-828-3251 or visit the website at www.nps.gov/gumo.

Hueco Tanks (Texas)

Just 32 miles from El Paso (roughly 40 minutes away in good traffic), Hueco Tanks State Historical Park is an oasis of granite and indigenous culture in a beautiful Southwest desert landscape. The rock formations are brilliant for rock climbing and bouldering, but even if your family doesn't climb, the area is worth a visit.

The name "Hueco Tanks" refers to the rock hollows that collect water here. They're particularly noticeable in the spring, when they are sometimes overflowing. The abundance of these rock features has long attracted aboriginal people to the area. Evidence of their occupation, in the form of cave paintings, is incredibly rich. In fact, anthropologists believe that the concentration of some types of artwork at Hueco Tanks, especially mask paintings, is unrivalled anywhere in the Southwest.

Unfortunately, several of these paintings have been defaced in modern times, as well as in not-so-modern times. Butterfield stagecoaches used to stop here on the route between San Francisco and St Louis, and at least a few of the passengers left etchings on the rock walls. Partly because of the ongoing damage and also because of the continual destruction of native vegetation and animals in the area, local authorities have clamped down fairly heavily on user privileges within the park. Gone are the days of free exploration and discovery.

On a plus note, this agglomeration of rock and desert wilderness is undoubtedly better cared for now than it has been for over 100 years. Visitors entering the park are shown a compulsory 20-minute video that tells the story of Hueco Tanks and — only in its final minutes — sets out the rules of the trail.

Self-guided access is permitted in a large portion of the park and camping is also allowed in some areas (for tents, trailers and RVs). Call 915-849-6684 for more information or write to: Hueco Tanks State Historical Park, 6900 Hueco Tanks Rd. #1, El Paso, Texas 79938.

Southwest Highways

There's a certain magic to driving in the American Southwest

Highways in the Southwest are tough to beat, anywhere or anytime. There's a certain magic to driving here that is hard to put into words. Maybe it's the incredible scenery. Perhaps it's the beautiful desert light, the vast open spaces or (depending on the route you choose) the allure of having the road all to yourself for an hour or more at a stretch.

We've endeavored to chronicle a few of our favorite Southwest highway drives in the next section. In general, driving these roads (and most others in the region) should be fairly straightforward and incident-free. However, it's worth paying attention to a few essential precautions before getting behind the wheel to ensure that your trips are as relaxing as possible.

The first — and very important — proviso is that you must travel with sufficient fuel, especially on some of the more remote roads. Gas stations are often far apart and finding yourself stranded on the road is simply not fun. Need we say more?

Be sure to fuel up before embarking into remote areas

Likewise, make sure that you travel with lots of water, both for drinking and in the event that the car radiator boils over. This is less likely now than in years gone by, but it's still possible — especially during really hot weather. Check that your spare tire is inflated, in good shape and easily accessible should you need to replace a flat. Make sure that you have a decent tool kit with you and bring along a good road map.

Finally, watch out for animals that may wander onto the road at any time of day, but especially at dawn and dusk. Wild burros and deer are the most likely offenders, but you might also come across coyotes, antelope or even horses (especially in the Monument Valley area).

So long as you keep your wits about you, you'll likely find the driving here is a pure joy, more so than almost anywhere else. Drive safely — and have fun!

Zion to Kanab on Highway 9 and Highway 89 (Utah)

Almost from the moment you exit Zion National Park, the signature red rock mountains are replaced by a rolling, golden landscape. Highway 9 will take you to an intersection near a somewhat decrepit trailer park, where you can either turn north toward Bryce Canyon National Park or south toward Kanab.

Heading south immediately takes you back into that classic, Southwest red rock landscape. Along the way, you'll see the Moqui Caves (about six miles past the highway exit for Coral Pink Sand Dunes State Park), which are thought to be about 140 million years old. As you get closer to Kanab, the red rock landscape takes the form of small and medium-sized bluffs that are much "crumblier" than those you might have seen in Zion.

American Southwest

Kanab to Lee's Ferry on Highway 89A (Utah and Arizona)

Stretching from Kanab to Jacob's Lake, Highway 89A reaches an elevation of nearly 8,000 feet above sea level, snaking through the high country and a dense forest of ponderosa pines. On the way, you'll pass a junction with a road that leads to the north rim of the Grand Canyon. Unless it's your intention to travel there, stay to the left.

If everything suddenly feels very "northern" all of a sudden, just wait. You'll soon arrive at several roadside rest stops that look out over layers of distinctly red and white buttes and mesas.

This is not a heavily traveled highway, which makes it a nice reprieve from the busier Zion Parkway. From Jacob's Lake, the road becomes very curvy as you descend into an area of crumbly white rock and through lots of juniper trees. Soon, the stunning Vermilion Cliffs will come into view. The road heads steeply downhill as you leave Kaibab National Forest. Once it reaches the valley floor, it stretches out again — flat and straight.

As the road approaches Vermilion Cliffs, you'll pass a little settlement called Cliff Dwellers. This place should immediately grab the kids' attention. Surrounded by massive red boulders that seem to have rolled down off the surrounding mesa, it's a Mars-like environment. The settlement of Vermilion Cliffs, with a few neat cafés and shops, is a quaint spot in the midst of what seems like a dinosaur playground.

Turn left toward Lee's Ferry at Marble Canyon. The surrounding area is like a "mini Monument Valley", with boulders

Great camping near Lee's Ferry

Colorado River as viewed from Navajo Bridge

The town is historically significant and boasts stunning, red rock canyon scenery where the majestic Colorado River flows through high-ridged gorges. This is the safest place to cross the Colorado River for 700 miles and has been used by native people for centuries for that purpose.

The nearby desert contains numerous dry washes for the kids to explore. The River Trail is also a good hiking option for families. The two-mile route (round trip) starts from the launch ramp and runs along an old wagon road on its way to the upper ferry crossing, passing an old fort on the way. It should take you a little more than an hour to complete this hike.

balancing on smaller rocks in a seemingly precarious manner by the side of the road. To the right, you'll see the giant chasm that the Colorado River flows through.

Lee's Ferry

If you're trying to see as much of the Southwest as you can within a short time-frame, Lee's Ferry might seem a little too far off the beaten path to bother with it. Not so.

Just east of Lee's Ferry, you'll come to the Navajo Bridge Interpretive Center, which is open between April and October. Stop for a few moments to peer down from the old bridge that was built in 1928. It's an awesome experience. The Colorado River snakes its way beneath you, shaded by massive canyon walls. River rafters can be seen occasionally as they rush underneath.

Outside the interpretive center, you'll often

Route 66

Nat King Cole sang about it. A 1960s television show based adventures around it. A nation romanticized it. Route 66 became America's most famous highway when it was completed in the 1930s.

The 376 miles of pavement in Arizona represented a "road to a better life" after the travails of the Great Depression. The route strung together a series of towns that embodied a "Main Street of America" perspective. Roadhouses, scenic sites and historic buildings were meant to entice Americans to see the best their country had to offer.

Today, some of the original Route 66 is still intact. The best-preserved section is between Seligman and Topock. Along this section are the Grand Canyon Caves, where tours will take you 21 storeys underground.

If you drive this road west to Kingman, visit the Route 66 Museum. If you're heading toward Topock, stop at the "revived" ghost town of Oatman. Mom and dad can check out its funky art galleries and shops, while the kids feed the burros that walk freely around town.

find tables set up displaying Navajo jewelry for sale. Most of it is tasteful and inexpensive, and much of it caters to children.

The campsite at Lee's Ferry is one of only a few drive-in campsites on the Colorado River and is therefore a popular starting point for rafters. The campground has sheltered picnic tables, fire pits and well-maintained bathrooms. The closest motel and tourist services are available in Marble Canyon, located a few miles away.

From Lee's Ferry, continue east along Highway 89A to the junction with Highway 89. At this point, you can either drive north to Page or south toward Flagstaff.

For more information, call 928-608-6404 or check the website at www.nps.gov/glca/lferry.htm.

The open spaces of Highway 163, near Monument Valley

Page to Kaibito on Highway 98 (Arizona)

This steep drive leads to the Kaibito Plateau and offers outstanding views of the heart of Navajo territory. Since there are few towns on this route, there's also very little traffic.

On the way, you'll pass some interesting pinnacles on the right side of the road, about 25 miles out of Page. The ground cover in the area is largely rabbitbrush, which paints the desert yellow when it flowers in autumn. If any low-lying clouds appear, they'll likely appear mauve-colored in places. Ask the kids if they can guess why. (Answer: They're seeing a reflection of the red rock mountains below the clouds.)

Until it reaches the junction with Highway 160, the road winds through a series of red gorges and past clusters of juniper trees and cacti. The nearby rocks offer evidence of several geological periods and reveal interesting grey striations that wind through the

red sandstone.

Kaibito to Monument Valley on Highway 98, Highway 160 and Highway 163 (Arizona)

The traffic will likely intensify once you get onto Highway 160 and head northeast. Near Tsagi (a little town just before Kayenta), you'll get a glimpse of red rock canyon scenery followed by a view of impressive, free-standing pinnacles that rise up from the desert beyond Kayenta.

Unfortunately, this beautiful landscape isn't reflected in the nearby manmade structures. Kayenta is not what you'd call "pretty", although it does have the closest collection of family motels to Monument Valley.

As you turn onto Highway 163 at Kayenta,

the desert terrain becomes the stuff of old western movies and "coyote vs. road-runner" cartoons. Drive cautiously along this stretch. Wild horses roam through the area and often make their way onto the road. They're potentially dangerous and if you hit one, you'll have to contend with the Navajo justice system.

A couple of places at the side of the road offer horseback rides (see the Monument Valley sec-

If possible, stop for a moment just to take it all in

tion). The entrance to Monument Valley also features a number of quaint food and jewelry stalls of the sort you might see in Mexico. Instead of Mexican fare, however, the food being hawked here takes the form of Navajo tacos, mutton and fried bread.

Monument Valley to Moab on Highway 163 and Highway 191 (Arizona and Utah)

Road traffic is generally pretty light from Monument Valley to Mexican Hat. The scenery is dominated by roadside gorges that are fashioned from broken rock, and mesas with grey and mauve sandstone swirls. Mexican Hat is named after a red rock formation north of town that has one rock that looks like a sombrero balanced on top of a much smaller rock. The town has a few shady motels and gas stations, but little else to offer.

After Mexican Hat, the scenery consists mainly of high, distant mesas. Sagebrush is pretty much the only other significant feature here, except for the occasional red rock pinnacle. The best examples are just north of the town of Bluff. Look for the Navajo Twin Rocks, just off to the left side of the road.

There are a few nice family motels situated in Bluff. North of town, the red rock disappears altogether as the landscape changes to desert prairie and the road passes through the Ute Indian Reservation. The next community you'll encounter is Blanding. The amenities here are quite good, with family motels, a comprehensive visitor center and a dinosaur museum with exhibits that change annually.

Beyond the next town, Monticello, your kids should be able to tell you why Utah is nicknamed "The Beehive State". The very cool conical rock formations can be seen off the side of the highway.

The La Sal Mountains will come into view

Quirky road signs on the way from Phoenix to Sedona

road look like sculpted pottery. Arches National Park will soon appear in the distance and a jagged series of blood-red peaks marks the gateway to Moab, six miles to the north.

Phoenix (Camp Verde) to Sedona, Flagstaff and the Grand Canyon (Arizona)

Over a span of about 60 miles, this route will lead you into spectacular red rock country, through the beautiful town of Sedona (see the separate chapter on this intriguing town), through the shady and historic Oak Creek Canyon and past Flagstaff's lovely ponderosa pine forests and snow-capped mountains. Beyond that point, Highway 64 eventually takes you to the south rim of the Grand Canyon.

About eight miles north of Camp Verde on Highway 17 (northbound from Phoenix), you'll spot directional signs for Sedona. Turn left (west) on Highway 179 and drive 7.5 miles through red rock country to reach the outskirts of Sedona.

Stop to sample some of the delightful attractions this lovely town has to offer or stay overnight. Then continue north on Highway 89A. You'll drive through the heart of Oak Creek Canyon to begin with and then switchback your way up a rather steep section and through a pine forest on the final ascent to Flagstaff.

a few minutes later and pink rock mesas start to appear, with much smoother faces than you may have seen in either Zion National Park or Monument Valley. Many of the formations that you can see from the

In Flagstaff, look for signs indicating the turnoff for Highway 180 (northbound). Follow this road through beautiful pine and juniper forests for about 30 miles to the intersection with Highway 64. The Grand Canyon is located further north to the right.

Southwest Driving Circuits

America's Southwest is about the size of Western Europe, which means that you'll have to hit the road to explore it. Fortunately, the range of adventure opportunities along the highway is as vast as the landscape that surrounds it.

You never know what you'll be tempted to do while driving through the Southwest

Several major airports service cities in the Southwest, as well as many smaller ones. Here are some of our favorite driving circuits) that start from those cities and include great "home bases" to spend a few days in, plus the scenic routes that link them together. Try to allow at least two weeks for each of these routes — and more if you can manage it.

Circuit from Los Angeles

This circuit offers a little bit of everything when it comes to Southwest landscapes. You'll ascend from the deserts of Death Valley to the lower slopes of Mount Whitney, and travel from the funky forests of Joshua Tree National Park to the colorful magic of Red Rock Canyon State Park.

Day 1: Drive to Joshua Tree National Park or Twentynine Palms via Highway 10 and Highway 62.

Day 2 and 3: Explore Joshua Tree National Park.

Day 4: Drive to Death Valley via Highway 127. Stay in Death Valley or at Stovepipe Wells.

Day 5: Explore Death Valley.

Day 6: Explore Death Valley.

Day 7: Drive to Lone Pine via Highway 190. Stay in Lone Pine.

Day 8: Explore the Mount Whitney area. Stay in Lone Pine.

Day 9 and 10: Drive to Bishop via Highway 395. Explore Inyo National Forest, the Buttermilks and other nearby attractions. Stay in Bishop.

Day 11: Drive to Red Rock

Descending into Death Valley from the west

ers. At the heart of the trip is a three-day exploration of Lake Powell by houseboat. Then it takes you through the majesty of Monument Valley and the Grand Canyon before you return to Las Vegas. Allocating more than two weeks to this trip will give you additional time to explore some of the numerous tributary roads en route.

Day 1: Drive to Springdale.
Day 2: Explore Zion National Park.
Day 3: Explore Zion National Park.
Day 4: Drive to Kanab via Highway 9 and Highway 89. Visit Coral Pink Sand Dunes State Park. Stay in Kanab.
Day 5: Drive to Lee's Ferry via Highway 89. Stay at a campground in Lee's Ferry.
Day 6: Drive to Page via Highway 89. Rent a houseboat and explore Lake Powell.
Day 7 and 8: Explore Lake Powell.
Day 9: Return by boat to Page and drive to Monument Valley via Highway 98, Highway 160 and Highway 163.
Day 10: Explore Monument Valley. Stay at a campground or in near Kayenta.
Day 11: Drive to the Grand Canyon via Highway 160, Highway 89 and Highway 64.

Canyon State Park via Highway 395 and Highway 14.
Day 12: Explore Red Rock Canyon State Park.
Day 13: Head back to L.A.

Circuit from Las Vegas

The beauty of this circuit is its variety. It includes stops at red rock canyons and pink sand dunes and walks through dry desert gorges and alongside raging whitewater riv-

Driving past the "goblins" of Goblin Valley State Park, Utah

Day 12: Explore the Grand Canyon on foot or by mule. Stay in Grand Canyon National Park or Tusayan.

Day 13: Drive back to Las Vegas via Highway 64, Highway 40 and Highway 93.

Circuit from Phoenix

This is a quintessential "Arizona" circuit that will give you a small taste of the many adventures this fine state has to offer and then leave you wanting more.

Day 1: Drive from Phoenix to Ajo via Highway 10 and Highway 85.

Day 2: Explore Organ Pipe Cactus National Monument. Stay in Ajo.

Day 3: Drive to Tucson via Highway 86 and stay overnight in Tucson.

Day 4 and 5: Explore Tucson Mountain Park, Saguaro National Park and other attractions in the Tucson area.

Day 6: Drive to Tombstone via Highway 10 and Highway 80. Stay in Tombstone.

Day 7: Drive to Picacho Peak State Park via Highway 80 and Highway 10. Explore the park and then camp there overnight.

Day 8: Drive to Sedona via Highway 10 and Highway 17. Stay in Sedona.

Day 9: Explore the Sedona area and stay there overnight.

Beautiful roads lead through cactus country near Tucson

Day 10: Drive to the Grand Canyon via Highway 89, Highway 40 and Highway 64.

Day 11: Explore the Grand Canyon.

Day 12: Drive to Monument Valley via Highway 64, Highway 89, Highway 160 and Highway 163. Stay in Monument Valley or in nearby Kayenta.

Day 13: Explore Monument Valley in the morning. In the afternoon, drive to Canyon de Chelly National Monument via Highway 163, Highway 160 and Highway 191. Stay in a motel or camp in Chinle.

Day 14: Explore Canyon de Chelly National Monument in the morning. Drive to Sedona via Highway 191, Highway 40 and Highway 89 in the late afternoon. This is the longest day of driving down a fairly uninteresting highway, so you won't miss much in the dark. Stay in Sedona.

Day 15: After a leisurely morning in Sedona, drive back to Phoenix via Highway 179 and Highway 17.

Grand Circle Circuit

This is the most popular driving circuit in the Southwest — and for good reason. Covering 1,300 miles in 14 days, the Grand Circle takes in most of the highlights of the region, including the Grand Canyon, Zion National Park, Bryce Canyon National Park, Capitol Reef National Park, Arches National Park, Canyonlands National Park and Monument Valley.

Day 1: Arrive in Las Vegas and drive to Springdale. If you're planning on camping for the next couple of weeks, you might want to consider stopping for one last prepared meal and dine out in style. In Mesquite, Nevada, there are a few casinos that offer great buffets at reasonable prices. A stop there will break up the drive and keep your kids' stomachs satisfied until they get to Springdale. There are a couple of good grocery stores in Hurricane, 21-miles west of Springdale) if you need to stock up on food.

Checking the map in Capitol Reef National Park

Day 2: Explore Zion National Park.

Day 3: Drive to Bryce Canyon National Park via Highway 89.

Day 4: Explore Bryce Canyon National Park.

Day 5: Drive to Capitol Reef National Park via Highway 12. If you can, stop along the way to check out Kodachrome Basin State Park and GrandStaircase-Escalante National Monument. Stay in Capitol Reef National Park.

Day 6: Drive to Moab via Highway 24, Highway 70 and Highway 191. Consider hiking one of the shorter walks (to Delicate Arch or Landscape Arch) before settling in for the evening.

Driving through acres of brightness in White Sands National Monument

Day 7: Explore Arches National Park.

Day 8: Drive to Canyonlands National Park via Highway 313. Stay in Moab.

Day 9: Drive to Monument Valley via Highway 191 and Highway 163. This is a fairly long day in the car, so look for nice places to stretch your legs. The Blanding Dinosaur Museum in Blanding is one suggestion. Stay in Monument Valley or in nearby Kayenta.

Day 10: Explore Monument Valley. Stay in Monument Valley or in nearby Kayenta.

Day 11: Drive to Grand Canyon National Park via Highway 160, Highway 89 and Highway 64. Stay in Grand Canyon National Park or Tusayan.

Day 12: Explore Grand Canyon National Park. Stay in Grand Canyon National Park or Tusayan.

Day 13: Drive back to Las Vegas via Highway 64, Highway 40 and Highway 93.

Eastern Southwest Circuit

Santa Fe, Albuquerque and El Paso are all suitable starting points for this circuit. Whichever you choose, feel free to vary each day's activities and the overnight stays to suit your family. We've chosen Santa Fe as our starting point and ending point here.

Day 1 to 3: Explore Santa Fe and the surrounding area, in as much depth as you like.

Day 4: Drive south past Albuquerque on Highway 25 and continue past Socorro. Then drive east on Highway 380 to Carrizozo. Turn right and head south on Highway 54 to Alamogordo, stopping (at least briefly) in Tularosa. Stay in Alamogordo.

Day 5 and 6: Let the kids blow off some steam (and enjoy yourself, too) at White Sands National Monument.

Day 7: Drive south on Highway 54 and then Highway 375 (around El Paso) to reach Highway 62. Turn left (east) and continue on to Hueco Tanks State Historical Park.

Day 8: Spend the day bouldering or hiking around the Tanks. Camping is great here.

Day 9: Drive east on Highway 62 to Guadalupe Mountains National Park. Spend the afternoon hiking and then camp over-night here.

Day 10 and 11: Drive on to Carlsbad Caverns National Park. Explore as much of the cave system as you have time for and then spend the night nearby.

Day 12: Drive back to Santa Fe via Highway 285.

Safe travels! (and hopefully uneventful, too...)

Kid's Stuff

The possibility of discovering new things while hiking along a creek bed, exploring a deep canyon or traversing a ridge crest will motivate most kids at the outset of a trip.

If the mere thought of traveling with energetic kids threatens to derail even your best-conceived vacation plans, take heart in the knowledge that you're not alone. We had many second thoughts before heading out on our first overseas trip with a toddler in tow. Other parents we've met since have confessed their initial reluctance to do the same. Some told us that they didn't really believe that travel (other than the "packaged" sort) was possible with young children.

While it's true that really rambunctious kids — or those demanding constant stimulation — may pose a serious challenge to traveling parents, kids generally respond well to the forced routine of a trip. Most kids appreciate travel's merits quickly and learn to cope (almost as rapidly) with the less-active periods that are also part of the travel experience.

Taking your children on a trip need not be a fearful enterprise. If you're like us, the main concern might be ensuring that their travel experience is as rewarding as possible. This

Buying or taking along an inexpensive glider can be a great (and fun) investment while on the road

requires some creativity, planning and serious forethought. Using the right approach, however, can make the difference (in any youngster's mind) between a boring time spent with parents and a truly exciting adventure.

The following section looks at ways of entertaining kids while on the road and making activities like hiking (which might seem a little humdrum at first) downright enjoyable. It also suggests some recipes to try if you have a kitchen to work in on more relaxed days, or after a few hours of strenu-

ous activity.

Entertainment Ideas:

It's inevitable that at some point you'll be driving down a foreign highway adhering to very foreign rules of the road, and listening to this not-so-foreign chatter from the back seat: "I'm bored." "How much longer till we get there?" "So-and-so just pinched me."

At times such as these, having a secret bag of tricks on hand — or at least a bag full of

You won't need extra activities for the kids on roads such as this; save them for the flat, boring stretches

games — can be invaluable. Here are some of our tried and true favorites that, in a pinch, may help avoid that pinch...

The Alphabet Game

Name countries, foods, animals, etc. that start with the letters A to Z. Establish a time limit and a "three strikes and you're out" rule.

I Spy

his is a classic car game, especially when you're driving through an area as richly colored as red rock canyons are in spring. "I spy, with my little eye, something that is green..."

I Packed My Bag

"I packed my bag and in it I took..." This is an old summer camp favorite. Take turns saying this initial phrase, adding one extra item per person until someone can't remember the full list.

Who Am I?

One player thinks of a well-known person or animal and the other players have to guess who or what it is. Players take turns asking questions that can only be answered with "yes" or "no".

Rock, Paper, Scissors

Each player forms a fist. On the count of "three", the competitors unveil two out-stretched fingers (i.e. scissors), a flat hand (paper) or the same fist (rock). "Rock smashes scissors, scissors cut paper and paper covers rock" is the rule. One point is given for each win. Play up to 10 points.

Truth or Lie?

Have someone say five things about themselves, with one of them being a lie. The truth is learned by gradually figuring out which four claims are fiction and which single claim is fact.

At your home base...

- Hold a treasure hunt.
- If you have a decent kitchen available, make dinner and/or desserts that are characteristic of the region you're traveling in. (See the sample recipes below.)
- Create your own boardgame, such as variations on Snakes & Ladders, Trivial Pursuit, etc.
- Get the kids to look at a local map and help you plan the next day's trip.
- Other great games are available on the Internet at: www.familyeducation.com.
- Print out some paper airplane designs from: www.paperairplanes.co.uk.

Other Activities in the Car

Spot the Car

Ask the kids to identify different makes or colors of cars. The first person to reach 10 of the chosen type wins. This game is especially fun around ritzy places like Sedona, where cars tend to be more exotic. Make Hummers and other unusual vehicles worth more points!

Laptop Movies

If you have a laptop computer with a built-in DVD player, movies can be a great option for longer road trips. Just make sure that your power cord adapter will plug into the lighter socket, or else ensure that your computer battery will last through the whole show — or else!

Audio Book Cassettes or CDs

Books on audio tape or CD are readily available at roadside service stations in the U.S. They offer a great way to keep your kids occupied while away on holiday.

Journeys with Kids: Travel Games & Journal

For a more comprehensive selection of "boredom busters", pick up a copy of Journeys with Kids: Travel Games & Journal. The book contains dozens of games to teach your kids about the wonders of travel, while entertaining them at the same time. The book also contains journal pages so that travel memories can be preserved and read again years from now. (The first edition of this book will be published by March, 2007.)

Trail Psychology

If your kids are anything like ours, getting them up a hiking trail is not always an easy task. The inevitable whines of "I'm tired" or "This is boring" or "How long till we get there?" will take a toll on even the most patient and persistent parents.

If things are starting to fall apart on the trail, it's worth taking a break to turn the situation around. Friends of ours have one trick they swear by when they're out hiking with children who are getting tired. One parent will run ahead during a rest break to place candies at set intervals on the next stretch of trail. The other parent then gives the revitalized youngsters clues for finding the candy.

"Trail blues" can also be alleviated in ways that might not be as obvious as a treasure hunt for candy. A little foresight can go a long way once you're underway, as can basic child psychology. The next section covers proven techniques that we've used while blazing trails in the Southwest with our own kids.

Choose routes that are fun

This may seem like an obvious strategy at first, but it's overlooked by many parents (and by us from time to time). Select fun paths to hike with your kids! Narrow and winding tracks are best, if not always easy to find. Look for trails that offer frequent rewards, such as great views or — even better — scrambles along rocky ridgelines or to the top of a small crest.

Avoid routes that involve long, tedious slogs through relatively uninteresting forest or scrub areas, especially if the paths tend to be wide, flat and straight. There's no more certain way to wear down the enthusiasm of even the keenest kids (and adults, for that matter) than a boring trek through the woods.

We've tried to select routes for this book that minimize boring stretches of trail, in favor of ones with more immediate appeal. When tedious travel is unavoidable for more than a few minutes, our routes have to pass one of two litmus tests, as described below.

Outings with an ulterior motive

The possibility of discovering new things while hiking along a creek bed, exploring a deep canyon or traversing a ridge crest will motivate most kids at the outset of a trip. My parents cajoled me and my four siblings into hiking up dozens of mountain trails, either with the promise of a teahouse serving fresh scones and hot chocolate, or a great little fishing hole at the other end. (We rarely caught anything, as you can imagine, with five rowdy kids clamoring along the lakeshore.)

Kids naturally differ in terms of what keeps them going once they get started. Nonetheless, there are some basic techniques that work for most children. Eating freshly cooked treats is one, but the chance of spotting one or more wild desert animals runs a close second. Getting to the top of something — even a minor peak — is an energetic challenge that few kids can resist.

There's nothing like a game of "hide and seek" to break up the tedium of a hike

Biking is never so much fun as when there's terrain to jump over or dodge around

An exciting downhill stretch can be a great motivator, especially if combined with a rewarding uphill section. Rolling down a sand dune or "boot skiing" in steep scree (small rocks) usually makes a descent a lot more fun than merely pounding down a trail. Several of our itineraries provide options for fun descents.

Combining hiking with something else

Some of our suggested itineraries combine hiking with another adventure activity. Mountain biking is one that blends in easily, but a few routes offer options such as roped scrambling or climbing. Others may include a boat ride.

Even a short stretch of biking will break up the monotony of a long hike. Boating

Taking along a pair of climbing shoes for everyone can open up a range of new possibilities, even on a simple outing

to a trailhead (such as on Lake Powell) creates a sense of getting far away before the real physical work actually begins. Moreover, the return trip is also something to look forward to. An exciting climb is an enticement that keeps kids interested, even if the approach hike is fairly dull.

Of course, carrying along enough gear for dual activities is usually more work than for a simple hike, and might not be worth it in some cases. We wouldn't recommend renting bikes just for the short ride to the dinosaur tracks found near Moab, for example. But if you're transporting your own gear or have invested in a multi-day rental package, then biking a section of otherwise boring trail makes good sense.

SOUTHWESTERN RECIPES

Whether you're traversing the desert in an RV, pitching tents and cooking over a campfire, or preparing meals in the kitchenette of your motel, the following recipes are easy to make, tasty and kid-friendly. They're also representative of the region you're traveling through. (OK, maybe not the caramel corn and Smores…)

Simple Flour Tortillas
This recipe is where all Southwest cooking begins. As a strategy to get your kids involved with making meals, kneading tortilla dough is tough to beat. Better still, once the tortillas have been prepared, only your own creativity will limit what you can do with them. Try stuffing

scrambled eggs, refried beans and salsa inside them in the morning, or serve them with one of our recommended chilis (with cheese) for lunch or dinner.

4 cups	flour
2 tsp.	salt
½ cup	shortening
1¼ cups	lukewarm water

Sift flour and salt into a large bowl. Add shortening and mix well. Add lukewarm water and continue to blend. Place dough on a lightly floured surface and knead about 60 times. (Get the kids to help with this part!) Separate dough into 12 balls of equal size. Cover them with a cloth and let them stand for about 20 minutes. Form each ball into a round tortilla. If you don't have a roller, perhaps mom and dad have a wine bottle on hand that will do the

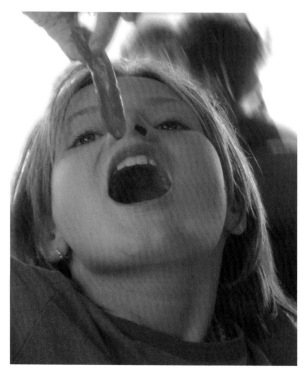

I dare you to down that jalapeno!

trick. Cook the tortillas in an ungreased skillet on low to medium heat, until tortillas start to turn golden. Flip over and repeat. Makes about a dozen tortillas.

Salsa Verde

10	small, ripe roma tomatoes, diced
½ cup	chopped red onion
¼ cup	minced fresh cilantro
2	jalapeño peppers, seeded and minced
2 tsp.	fresh lime juice
½ tsp.	salt
4	garlic cloves, crushed

This simple salsa, combined with home-made tortillas, provides the basis for almost any Southwest meal. Make sure that the jalapeño peppers are seeded before using them and taste the salsa as you go to make sure it's not too spicy for the children.

Southwest Buffalo Tostada

This is a classic Southwest finger food that's very popular with kids.

1 lb.	lean ground buffalo (beef works well, too)
1	large onion, chopped
1 can (16 oz)	kidney beans, drained
1½ tsp.	chili powder

½ tsp.	ground cumin
6 tbsp.	ketchup
5 cups	iceberg lettuce, shredded
1 cup shredded	Monterey Jack cheese,
2 large	tomatoes, chopped
	tortilla chips

Fry meat and onion in a large skillet until the meat's pink color is gone. Drain and discard the excess fat. (There won't be much, since buffalo meat is very lean.) Add kidney beans, chili powder, cumin and ketchup, and simmer for about five minutes. Cover dinner plates with lettuce and spread the cooked mixture on top. Next, sprinkle on the cheese and tomatoes. Serve with "scoop shaped" tortilla chips (available at grocery stores all over the Southwest) and enjoy — without forks!

Spicy Rattlesnake Chili

The key to this tasty and colorful chili is finding the rattlesnake meat. Some specialty meat stores in larger cities carry it. Otherwise, ground chicken, turkey or beef (although not as exotic) work well, too.

2 tbsp.	olive oil
1	onion, chopped
1	green pepper, chopped
1	red pepper, chopped
1	yellow pepper, chopped
3	garlic cloves, crushed
1½ lbs.	skinned, boned and diced rattlesnake
1 can (8 oz)	crushed tomatoes
1 can (16 oz)	tomato sauce
2 cans (16 oz.)	kidney beans
½ tsp.	cumin
½ tsp.	thyme
½ tsp.	sage
2 tbsp.	chili powder
pinch	salt
1 tbsp.	lime juice
1 cup	cheddar cheese, shredded

Heat up a big, cast-iron skillet over medium heat. Add oil, onion, peppers, garlic and salt. Sauté these ingredients for a few minutes and then put them aside on a plate. Over high heat, sauté the bite-sized pieces of rattlesnake with a little oil, lime juice and salt until the meat is thoroughly cooked. Return the cooked pepper mixture to the skillet and add the tomatoes, kidney beans, tomato sauce, chili powder, sage, cumin and thyme. Bring to a boil, reduce the heat, cover and let simmer for at least 30 minutes. Sprinkle shredded cheddar on top and serve with garlic toast.

Gunslinger Black Bean Chili

This chili can be served hot or cold and is incredibly easy to prepare. (Don't forget to drain and rinse the black beans before using them, or you'll regret it later in the tent!)

2 large cans	black beans, drained
2 small cans	corn kernels
1 large can	tomatoes
6	limes (juicy ones only)
1 head	garlic, crushed
2	bell peppers
1 tsp.	hot sauce
1 tbsp.	chili powder
	salt and pepper (to taste)

Add all of the ingredients to a large pot and let simmer for at least 30 minutes. How much garlic and hot sauce you use will depend on how much your kids like spicy food. Serve with a nice, hearty bread.

Breakfast Burrito

This is a family favorite that will put your homemade tortillas and salsa verde to good use!

1 tbsp.	butter
1	potato (medium-sized), finely diced

1	green bell pepper, seeded and finely diced
4 slices	bacon, cooked and crumbled
8	eggs, lightly beaten salt and fresh ground pepper to taste
4	flour tortillas, warmed
4 oz.	cheddar cheese, shredded
½ cup	salsa
2	scallions (green onions), finely chopped

Melt the butter in a skillet over moderate heat and sauté the potato and pepper until tender, about five minutes. Add the bacon and eggs and continue cooking, stirring frequently, until the eggs are set. Divide the egg mixture between the tortillas and top them with cheese, salsa and scallions.

Roll up the tortillas, tucking the ends under.

Campsite Caramel Corn

This is a simple recipe for a delicious treat that can be made right over the campfire. Remember to share — this stuff is tasty!

4 cups	unpopped popcorn
1 cup	unsalted almonds, roasted and chopped
½ cup	butter
¼ cup	light corn syrup
2/3 cup	sugar
½ tsp.	vanilla extract

Pop the popcorn and put it into a very large bowl. Add the nuts and set the bowl aside. In a separate pot, bring butter, corn syrup and sugar to a boil. Reduce to medium heat and continue to cook, stirring constantly, for about 12 minutes. When it turns a light caramel color, remove it from the heat and add the vanilla. Pour the mixture over the popcorn and nuts and stir everything together with a spoon to make sure it's well-mixed.

Smores

The Southwest is all about camping (especially for kids), so there's one dessert we can't neglect to mention. Best of all, the ingredients for this classic fireside recipe are readily available at most campground supply stores. The quantities you'll need depend on how hungry you are.

marshmallows
Hershey's chocolate bars (or any other slab of milk chocolate or dark chocolate)
Graham Wafers

Roast the marshmallows over the campfire and put them on a Graham Wafer, along with a piece of chocolate. Take a second Graham Wafer and mash it down on top. It's as simple as that, but beware of the hot marshmallow innards!

Travel Essentials

The Southwest is a haven for campers, whether they're driving an RV or sleeping in tents.

Language

Although there is no "official" national language in the United States, English is by far the most widely spoken. That's also the case in the Southwest, although Spanish is spoken by a large percentage of the population as well. In New Mexico, Spanish (along with English) is an official language of that state and is therefore used in all government services and literature (tourist brochures, etc.).

Indigenous languages are also commonly spoken throughout the Southwest, especially Navajo. It's spoken by close to 180,000 people.

Communication

Pay phones are abundant in Southwest towns, especially at gas stations and convenience stores. Larger campgrounds often have pay phones, too. Local calls are cheap and have no time limit. For long distance and international calls, it's advisable to purchase a phone card from a pharmacy or gas station to get the best rates.

Don't forget to bring an adapter if arriving from outside of North America

Nevada

Las Vegas (including McCarran International Airport): 702

New Mexico

Everywhere: 505

Utah

Salt Lake City (including Salt Lake City International Airport): 801

Southern Utah (including St. George, Kanab and Springdale): 435

The telephone "country code" for the U.S. is "1". The following are area codes for the towns, regions and states covered in this book.

Arizona

Northern Arizona (including Sedona and Flagstaff): 928

Southeast Arizona (including Tucson and Ajo): 520

Southwest Arizona (including part of Phoenix): 623

Parts of Northern Phoenix and Scottsdale: 602

Parts of Eastern Phoenix: 480

California

Parts of Los Angeles (including Los Angeles International Airport — LAX): 310

Parts of Los Angeles (including most of Hollywood): 323

Parts of Los Angeles (including the business district): 213

Eastern California (including Twentynine Palms, Lone Pine and Bishop): 760

Colorado

Western Colorado (including Cortez): 970

Parts of Denver (including Denver International Airport): 303

Parts of Denver: 720

All of the bases covered in this book have Internet cafés and/or public libraries that provide Internet access. Internet access at cafés costs roughly the same as that in comparable surroundings in Europe, Canada and Australia. Internet access is free of charge at public libraries, but there are often lineups to use the computers and usage time may be limited.

Electricity

Electricity in the American Southwest is delivered at 110 to 120 volts, through standard two-prong or three-prong outlets like those found elsewhere in North America. Europeans and some other visitors will need to use voltage adapters for any electronic devices they bring from home.

Adapters that convert 220-240 volts to 110-120 volts are difficult to find in this region (except perhaps at airports), so it's best to bring one along if you need one.

Business Hours

Most shops and services in the Southwest

are open from approximately 9 a.m. to 5 p.m. (or 6 p.m.) in the winter and from 9 a.m. to 9 p.m. in the summer. Hours will vary depending on the region you're in and what day it is.

Banks are typically open between 8 a.m. and 5 p.m., Monday to Friday, with some Saturday openings as well. Automated Teller Machines (ATMs) are common in larger communities and are generally open 24 hours per day.

Entry Requirements

All visitors to the United States must be able to provide proof of citizenship of their own country. Citizens and permanent residents of Canada are technically able to enter the U.S. without a passport, since a birth certificate and photo identification (such as a driver's licence) are generally accepted instead. However, we highly recommend carrying a passport, especially in this age of increased border security.

Children should either have passports of their own or be clearly identified in a parent's passport. If you're coming to the U.S. from Canada without a passport, be sure to at least carry birth certificates for your kids.

A passport alone is sufficient for visitors from most European nations (and current or former Commonwealth countries), but make sure it isn't going to expire within six months of your arrival or you'll be denied entry.

For up-to-date entry requirements, contact the nearest United States embassy or consulate, or check the U.S. State Department travel website (www.travel.state.gov) or

the U.S. Department of Homeland Security website (www.dhs.gov).

Etiquette and Customs

Gratuities (tips) are generally expected for satisfactory service in restaurants, cafés and bars. Typically, a tip should be about 15 per cent of the bill, with a higher percentage offered for truly exemplary service. Housekeepers, bellhops, concierges, tour guides and taxi drivers are some of the other service providers who customarily receive a tip for their assistance.

Children are not permitted in pubs or taverns in the United States. The U.S. has the highest legal drinking age in the world, at 21 years old.

It's illegal for anyone under the age of 18 to buy tobacco, including cigarettes. Smoking is banned in most workplaces and public buildings. In California, smoking is also prohibited in restaurants and bars. Smoking restrictions are less strict in other areas of the Southwest. However, some places (such as Albuquerque and Flagstaff) are starting to follow California's lead. Check with the proprietor of the establishment before lighting up.

Accommodations

For most recommended "base" towns, we've included telephone numbers for accommodation assistance under the heading of Other Resources. Calling those phone numbers will put you in touch with people who can help you find the most appropriate lodgings for your family, whether it's a campground, a bed and breakfast (B&B), an apartment or a four-star hotel.

For those interested in taking their home on the road with them, consider renting an RV in one of the Southwest's larger cities. Las Vegas is a particularly affordable place to rent a camper van or larger vehicle. The biggest (and one of the cheapest) RV rental companies is Cruise America. Reservations can be made online at www.cruiseamerica.com.

Other research sources that will help you plan an upcoming trip include:

Southwest

www.nps.gov
(links for national parks and monuments in the region)
www.reserveusa.com
(U.S. Forest Service campgrounds)
www.aaa.com
(maps, travel advice and roadside assistance for American Automobile Association members, with contact information for AAA offices in Phoenix, Salt Lake City, Tucson, Albuquerque, Santa Fe and other large centers)
www.americansouthwest.net
(information on accommodations and attractions in the region)
www.cybercaptive.com
(Internet cafés in the region)

California

www.ca.gov
(state government)
www.parks.ca.gov
(state parks)

Utah

www.utah.com
(state travel advice)
www.utah.gov

Accommodation in the Southwest is often as interesting as it is varied

(state government)
www.nr.utah.gov
(state campgrounds)

Arizona

www.az.gov
(state government)
www.pr.state.az.us
(state parks)

New Mexico

www.newmexico.org
(state travel advice)
www.nmparks.com
(state parks)

Park Entry Fees and Campground Fees

The Southwest is a haven for campers, whether they're driving an RV or sleeping in tents. Despite this, there isn't a well-developed reservation system in place. Exceptions are facilities on the rims of the Grand Canyon, where bookings are sometimes required two months in advance. To make a reservation there using a credit card, call 800-365-2267.

Most campsites are operated on a "first come, first served" basis and are busy every night of the week in the peak season. You should plan to arrive early (perhaps 9 or 10 a.m.) to get a spot, especially at popular campgrounds in national parks.

Campsites in the Southwest, such as this one, may cost nothing at all

If you're planning to visit a few national parks while in the Southwest, it's worthwhile picking up an annual pass. You can purchase one at park information centers or by going to the website at www.nationalparks. org. The pass covers the park entry fee for the driver, one vehicle and the driver's family — all for $50 per year. (Campsites and parking cost extra, however.) The entrance fee for an individual park usually costs about $20.

Public campgrounds in designated national and state parks, monuments and forests usually have tent sites, toilets and a water supply. An overnight stay typically costs $10 to $25. Backcountry camping is often available (and is usually free) in national forests or on sites falling within the jurisdiction of the Bureau of Land Management. Check with a local ranger station to find out where sites are available.

Holidays and Special Events

Christmas Day and New Year's Eve are the biggest holidays in the American Southwest, as they are elsewhere in North America. December 25 (Christmas Day), December 26 (Boxing Day) and January 1 (New Year's Day) are public holidays. Banks, government offices and many other businesses will be shut on those dates. Parks are sometimes closed to the public on those dates as well.

On Christmas Eve (December 24), families and friends traditionally congregate in churches or in their homes. On New Year's Eve (the night of December 31), many of those same people will get together in restaurants or bars to celebrate the arrival of the new year.

Another major holiday period is the Easter long weekend, at the end of March or in early April. Good Friday is a national holiday. Independence Day (July 4) is an especially fun time to be in the Southwest, since many towns —even small ones — hold parades and have fireworks displays.

Other American holidays include Martin Luther King Jr. Day (the third Monday in January), President's Day (the third Monday in February), Memorial Day (the last Monday in May), Labor Day (the first Monday in September), Columbus Day (the second Monday in October), Veterans' Day (November 11) and Thanksgiving Day (the fourth Thursday in November).

Cinco de Mayo (May 5) celebrates Mexico's 1862 victory over the French and the holiday is observed in most Southwest towns with strong Hispanic heritage. Expect to see a parade or festival on that day, usually with tasty Mexican food and piñatas on hand for the kids.

Weather

The Southwest's climate is as diverse as its topography. Low-altitude desert regions can reach temperatures of well over 100º F in the summer, while high-altitude mountain areas can drop to well below freezing in winter. A rule of thumb: a 1,000-foot gain in elevation equals the same change in temperature experienced traveling 300 miles north.

The southern and western parts of Arizona lie below 3,000 feet and are typically very hot in the summer. All of New Mexico (except parts of the Rio Grande Valley and

Bright, sunny skies are the norm throughout the Southwest, with the occasional storm

the Pecos River Valley) is above 4,000 feet, making it much cooler year-round.

Most of Utah is over 6,000 feet, meaning that it can get even cooler than New Mexico. The exception is the southern part of the state (including Kanab and Springdale), where elevations are typically below 4,000 feet.

Eastern California is home to the highest and lowest points of land in the continental U.S., with Mt. Whitney (at 14,496 feet) remarkably close to Death Valley (at 282 feet below sea level).

What to Wear

The dress code throughout most of the Southwest is casual and "outdoorsy", although you might want to jazz things up a bit in parts of Sedona and some of the larger cities. If you're planning on doing a lot of camping, make sure that you and the kids bring clothes that you can layer.

Even in southern Arizona, a sweater or medium-weight jacket is advisable during the winter, since nighttime temperatures are known to dip more than 30º F from those experienced at midday. At higher elevations (even during the summer), a heavier jacket, toques and gloves will often come in handy.

During the warmer months, make sure you protect yourself against sunburn and sunstroke; use sunscreen (at least 30 SPF), a wide-brimmed hat and sunglasses. Water bottles (with a minimum capacity of one quart per person) are essential for hikes and bike rides. Hiking shoes with good soles are useful, especially in places where there's lots of rocky terrain.

Americans tend to dress less formally than Europeans for most occasions. In the evening, nice restaurants will expect guests to wear appropriate attire (long pants and collared shirts for men, with knee-length skirts or formal slacks for women). If in doubt, wear something comparable to what you'd wear at a restaurant in your own hometown.

Before You Go

In addition to buying insurance and making sure that everyone is healthy before traveling (see the "Health and Safety" section below), a little pre-departure planning is always wise.

When to Go

Once you've determined which season of the year you'd like to visit the Southwest, you'll want to decide which specific weeks or months you'd like to go. Your trip may coincide with your kids' school holidays, especially those in the summer, at Christmas or during the spring break.

If you have a little more flexibility in your schedule, then the weather might become a major factor as you decide on your itinerary. It can be difficult to time a trip exactly right for your preferred outdoor activities (especially given the vagaries of the weather), but some bets are safer than others.

If you want to travel over the Christmas break and your family enjoys mountain biking and hiking, then head to southern or western Arizona — where it's warm enough to wear T-shirts and shorts on most days. During this same time of the year, Utah, New Mexico, Eastern California and Northern Arizona also offer quality skiing opportunities.

The summer months of July and August can be scorching hot in southwestern Arizona,

Some parts of the Southwest, such as Death Valley, are best avoided in the summer months when temperatures are often unbearable

but it's high season for tourists elsewhere in the region — thanks to the fact that most school holidays in North America and Europe coincide with that period.

Spring is a quieter time for tourism and Mother Nature can serve up either good or poor weather conditions. March and April can be mild and bring beautiful displays of desert wildflowers, but they can also be chilly. You may also come across flooded areas, thanks to runoff from higher elevations.

For many people, the months of September and October are the best time of the year to travel to the Southwest. There are usually moderate temperatures throughout the region, smaller crowds of tourists and impressive fall colors.

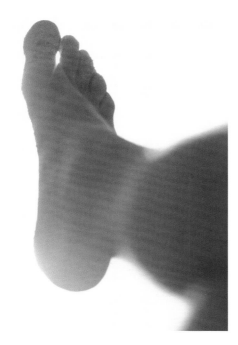

Going barefoot works in some places, but you'll need sturdy footwear and outer gear for most of the activities we recommend

Packing Your Bags

The following are basic lists of items you'll likely need for an adventure holiday in the American Southwest. If you don't already have some of these things at home, you can always buy them once you arrive.

For a Summer Visit
• Fleece clothing and windbreakers for everyone.
• Shorts and long pants (perhaps with zip-off pant legs)
• Sturdy hiking boots or walking shoes for everyone, along with light, quick-dry socks
• Backpacks for Mom and Dad, with small packs for the kids
• Camping gear, if you plan on car camping or embarking on hikes of several days' duration
• Climbing or biking gear, if those are your preferred activities
• Emergency medical kit (see below) with extra Band-Aids for scrapes picked up on the trail
• Sun protection (sunglasses, hats and sunscreen for everyone)
• Swimsuits, sandals and towels for lake or river excursions

For a Winter Visit
• Heavy fleece clothing and (if you're visiting mountainous areas) parkas, toques and gloves for everyone
• Insulated hiking boots (in southern Arizona, strong-soled hiking shoes are fine)
• More spare socks than you'd normally bring, especially heavyweight ones
• Backpacks to carry lunches and extra items of clothing on hikes or trips up the ski hill
• Emergency medical kit (see below) with support bandages for twists or strains
• Sunglasses and sunscreen (This is especially important for spring skiing or if you're visiting southern Arizona.)

Getting There

By Air

Depending on where you plan to do the bulk of your traveling, several international airports provide quick access to the Southwest.

If the Sierra Nevada, Death Valley and Joshua Tree National Park are your priorities, fly into Los Angeles International Airport (LAX). If southern Utah (including Zion National Park) is your first planned stop, fly into McCarran International Airport in Las Vegas (www.mccarran.com). If Moab or Bryce Canyon National Park are top attractions, then head for Salt Lake City (www.slcairport.com).

For Sedona, Monument Valley and Canyon de Chelly National Monument, the Sky Harbor airport in Phoenix will work well. (www.phxskyharbor.com). For southern Arizona, Tucson International Airport provides the most direct access (www.tucsonairport.org).

Travel to New Mexico is best done either by flying to Albuquerque or to Denver, Colorado, which is just a few hours away by car from northern New Mexico.

The Southwest's airports are not as well-served by direct flights from Europe or Asia as other regions in the U.S. In most cases, visitors from those regions will have to transfer to a domestic flight from major hubs such as Los Angeles, San Francisco, Chicago or Dallas. Las Vegas is starting to break that pattern, with direct flights now arriving regularly from London and Tokyo.

Once you're in the Southwest, your best bets for cheap regional flights are smaller carriers like America West (www.americawest.com) or Southwest Airlines (www.south-west.com). Both airlines offer low-cost, one-way fares — and discounts for kids.

By Car

Driving in the U.S. is a treat. There's an extensive and well-maintained road system, and fuel prices here are far cheaper than those in Europe, Australia or Canada. Signing up for a membership in the American Automobile Association (AAA) might be worthwhile for some travelers. For about $40 per year, you'll have access to an inexpensive roadside assistance service and all the maps of the Southwest you could ever want.

If you're arriving from the north, a few main highways lead right to the Southwest. Interstate 5 runs down through the western states, from the Canadian border all the way to Los Angeles (with a total travel time of about 20 hours). Interstate 15 runs through Utah and Nevada on the way to Los Angeles. (A trip from Salt Lake City to Las Vegas takes about seven hours.) Interstate 25 runs through Colorado and the heart of New Mexico, with a trip from Denver to Albuquerque taking about 7½ hours.

From the west, take Highway 10 from LA to Phoenix (seven hours) and then on to New Mexico (14 hours to Albuquerque). If you're coming from the east, Highway 40 runs from Texas through New Mexico and Arizona, on the way to California. (The Dallas-to-Phoenix run takes about 17 hours.)

From the south, the main points of entry from Mexico are Mexicali (near San Diego), Nogales (to reach Phoenix or Tucson) and El Paso/Ciudad Juárez (to get to Tucson and Albuquerque). It will take you about 4½ hours to drive from Puerto Penasco (using Mexico Highway 8) to Phoenix.

For a detailed overview of roads and driving times from Mexico, check the website at www.virtualmex.com.

Getting Around

If you plan to see a lot of the Southwest, it's a good idea to rent a car or a recreational vehicle (RV). Even if you just want to establish one "home base" and then take side

Ballooning is an unique — and spectacular — way to see the Southwest

trips, a vehicle will help you quickly get to trailheads and other local attractions we've recommended.

A rental vehicle with four-wheel-drive (4WD) capability makes sense if you're traveling in mountainous areas during the winter, since the roads can be slippery with snow and ice. A 4WD vehicle is also helpful for navigating dirt roads in places such as Monument Valley or around Moab, at any time of the year.

The cost of renting a vehicle in the United States is comparable to that found in Canada, but cheaper than in Europe or Australia.

Major roads in the Southwest can get very busy at times (especially during the high season near popular attractions such as Sedona and the entrances to national parks), but they're almost all paved and well-maintained. In the low season, your vehicle may be the only car in sight for long stretches. (See the

Southwest Highways section.)

Drivers are generally courteous, especially if you're accustomed to driving in Europe! It's always a good idea to check weather forecasts and current road conditions before setting off, particularly in mountainous areas during the winter.

Thunderstorms occur frequently in the Southwest (especially in Arizona) between

Biking is another

July and September, and they can some-times make driving conditions hazardous. Heavy rains, combined with motor oil residue on the roads, can produce very slick conditions. Maintain a safe distance between your vehicle and other vehicles in case you need to make a sudden stop, and always observe the speed limit.

Dust storms are quite common in the Southwest. Walls of dust hundreds of feet high sometimes move through the valleys. Visibility can be reduced dramatically, so it's best to stay off the road at those times. Sudden downpours can also cause flooding. Always obey any road sign that warns driv-ers not to travel through a flooded area.

If you're traveling with an RV, be aware of your vehicle's limitations. Don't travel on dirt roads (in Monument Valley, for example) that will put at you at risk of get-ting stuck. Towing fees can be horrendously high.

Countless tour companies operate from the bases we've recommended in this book. In Moab, the offerings range from whitewater rafting tours to driving Hummers over red rock landscapes. In Springdale, you can go rock climbing or explore slot canyons. In Sedona, you can take a "vortex" tour or go on a guided mountain biking trip. In the Grand Canyon, companies offer guided pack mule expeditions. The possibilities are virtually endless. Check with the local tourist office, visitor center or chamber of commerce to see what tour will best suit your family's needs.

Public transit in Southwest cities may not be as well-developed as it is in larger U.S. cen-ters or in Europe. The schedules (especially on Sundays) can sometimes be irregular. Taxi fares vary from city to city, but expect to pay an average of about $2 per mile.

If your family enjoys bus travel, Greyhound is by far the most popular carrier between major Southwest cities and the smaller towns along the way. In New Mexico, the Greyhound subsidiary is called TNM&O. Fares for kids aged two to 11 are typically discounted at 40 per cent off the adult fare. Greyhound's North America Discovery Pass is a good option if you plan to tour the area for a month or longer. Check out your options online at www.greyhound.com or www.discoverypass.com.

Biking with kids on major highways is not a good idea. These roads tend to experience heavy traffic, dominated by tourists who are often too busy looking at the scenery to pay proper attention to the road. On smaller side roads, however, biking is often the best way to get around.

Health and Safety

The American Southwest is generally a very safe and healthy place to travel with your kids. The region's wide-open spaces and generally warm weather mean that even young children can explore the region in comfort.

As with any outdoor experience, however, parents always have to consider potential hazards. In the Southwest, that starts with protecting the family against dehydration or sunburn. If you're taking a day trip in a desert area — or even in the highlands during the summer — plan on carrying two quarts of water per person. Portable hydration systems like the "Camelback" are excellent options for extended hiking or biking trips. Sunscreen with a minimum protection level of SPF 30 should be applied even on cloudy days. Wide-brimmed hats and bandanas (to wick away sweat) are also advisable.

When riding bikes in areas where the rock is slick, always stay on the marked trails and never venture too far off the beaten path. Cliff edges in areas such as Moab can be hazardous. Bike helmets and safety glasses should always be worn.

The Southwest is home to a lot of rock that can crumble underfoot.

Several of the Southwest's smaller inhabitants can deliver a nasty bite, even if they're not poisonous

When trekking in steep areas, be aware of potential rockfalls caused by fellow hikers (or animals) on any trail or cliff above you. If in doubt, wear helmets and consult the ranger station or local tourist office about trail hazards.

The Southwest sometimes experiences potentially dangerous weather phenomena. Lighting strikes are very common during the "monsoon" season (generally during the summer months). If you suddenly find yourself in the middle of a severe lightning storm, crouch down in a dry depression in the ground and insulate yourself by putting your pack or some spare clothing between your body and the ground.

Flash floods are another thing to consider in wet months or during the late winter, after there's been heavy precipitation. Rain falling miles away can eventually make its way into a dry wash or canyon, and a wall of water several feet high can build up as it rushes rapidly downhill. These floods are stronger than they look. Water just a foot deep can easily knock over an adult. For more information, contact a local ranger station and watch out for warning signs in areas where flash floods occur.

Concerns about the Southwest's venomous creatures — rattlesnakes, scorpions, Gila monsters and insects such as black widows — are often overstated, but they are real nonetheless. The best way to avoid being bitten by any of these creatures is to conduct yourself responsibly in the animals' regular habitats. When exploring desert areas, watch where you're walking and don't turn over rocks where one of these animals could be seeking shelter from the sun. When climbing or scrambling up rocks, don't reach up into areas that are out of your line of sight. Always carry a snake-bite kit and first aid supplies when traveling in snake country.

As far as crime is concerned, the Southwest is one of the safer regions of North America. Keep an eye on the kids the same way you would at home and you should be fine. Pickpockets in major urban areas such as Los Angeles or Phoenix are probably the most prevalent crime concerns. Wearing a money belt around your waist or under

ally been enjoyable and trouble-free. We've also found that kids generally adapt well to time zone and climate changes — often better than their parents do.

However, a child's resistance to disease is lower than that of an adult. With some infections, a child's condition can deteriorate quite quickly if appropriate treatment isn't immediately available. Before taking children on a trip abroad, it's worth considering a few health fundamentals, including the following points.

Heaps of fresh air and exercise should make your trip to the Southwest an especially healthy one

your shirt is the best way to safeguard passports and other important documents. Always have photocopies of your passports and traveler's checks stashed away separately, just in case.

Healthy Traveling

Maintaining good health is often the most important issue for parents who travel with children. Our own experiences have usu-

Pre-departure Planning

Try to ensure that everyone stays healthy in advance of the trip. If you're traveling a long distance from home, resolve any outstanding medical issues first. If anyone in the family wears glasses (or contact lenses), take along a spare pair and a copy of the eyewear prescription.

If you or your kids require any special medications, be sure to take an adequate supply with you, since they may not always be available locally. It's wise to take along a photocopy of the prescription. Better still, bring along any packaging that indicates the generic name of the drug, rather than the brand name (which may not be available locally). That will allow you to obtain a replacement easier, as will carrying a letter from your doctor to prove that you can legally use the medication.

Health Insurance

It's always a good idea to purchase travel insurance that covers theft, loss and medical problems all in one policy. Your travel agent or insurance agent should be able to make a recommendation from the wide

A basic first aid kit will take care of simple injuries such as this one

variety of policies available. Alternatively, shop around on the Internet for a policy that best suits your needs.

Be aware that some policies offer a choice of lower or higher medical expense options. The higher ones are intended primarily for countries like the United States, where medical treatment costs are particularly steep. Check the small print carefully before committing to any policy.

Some insurance packages specifically exclude "dangerous activities", which may include mountain climbing, parasailing, trekking or even skiing. Be sure to read your policy carefully before undertaking any of these activities.

You may prefer to take out an insurance policy that pays doctors or hospitals directly, instead of one that asks you to pay for medical services on the spot and then submit a claim for the expenses later. If you have to make a claim later, make sure you hang onto all pertinent documentation from the onset of the illness or injury.

Note that some policies require you to call an administration centre in your home country when a mishap occurs, so an immediate assessment of your problem can be made. This is not necessarily a bad thing, but you should be aware of any such requirement. Finally, check to see if the policy covers the cost of an ambulance ride or an emergency flight home.

Medical Kit

Especially when you bring kids along on your travels, it makes good sense to assemble a small and straightforward medical kit before leaving home so you can carry it with you wherever you go.

At the very least, the kit should include:

• Aspirin or paracetamol (also known as acetaminophen in the U.S.): Used to alleviate pain or fever.
• Antihistamine (such as Benadryl): Used as a decongestant for colds and allergies, to ease the itching of insect bites or stings, and to help prevent motion sickness. There are several antihistamines on the market, each with its own pros and cons (e.g. a tendency to cause drowsiness). It's worth discussing your requirements with a pharmacist or doctor. Antihistamines may have sedative effects and may interact negatively with alcohol, so take care when using them.
• Antibiotics: These are useful if you're traveling well off the beaten track, but they must be prescribed. Be sure to carry a copy of the prescription with you.
• Loperamide (e.g. Imodium) or Lomotil: Used to treat diarrhea.
• Prochlorperazine (e.g. Stemetil) or metaclopramide (e.g. Maxalon): Used to treat nausea and vomiting.
• Rehydration mixture: Used for the treatment of severe diarrhea. This is particularly important when traveling with children in areas of dubious cleanliness, although this is not usually a concern in the American Southwest.
• Antiseptic, such as povidone-iodine (e.g. Betadine): Used to treat cuts and scrapes.
• Multivitamins: These supplements are especially handy on long trips, when dietary vitamin intake may be inadequate.
• Calamine lotion or aluminum sulphate spray (e.g. Stingose): Used to ease the irritation of insect bites and stings.
• Bandages and Band-Aids: Used for minor injuries.
• Moleskin, Second Skin or some other form of skin surface protection: This soft, cushioned material can be applied to heels and toes that have blistered while hiking. Sometimes it's helpful to cut a "doughnut hole" in a moleskin pad to

minimize direct contact with the sore area.
• Scissors, tweezers and a thermometer. Note that mercury thermometers are prohibited by airlines.
• Water purification tablets or iodine crystals. Follow the instructions carefully when using the latter.
• Cold or flu tablets, and throat lozenges. Pseudoephedrine hydrochloride (e.g. Sudafed) may be useful to avoid ear damage if you're flying and suffering from a cold or flu.

Other useful items include:

• Analgesic (e.g. Panadol)
• Anti-fungal treatments. (Especially for pre-existing fungal problems.)
• Anti-nauseants (e.g. Metoclopramide or Stemetil)
• Eczema cream. Useful if you or your kids are prone to eczema problems.
• Eye drops. Used as an emollient for dry eyes or for alleviating allergy symptoms.
• Insect repellent (DEET). We tend to carry this separately from the first aid kit to allow easy access, especially at the height of the mosquito season.
• Sunburn treatment, such as Aloe Vera. We keep lots of sunscreen close at hand while traveling anywhere in the desert. Sunburn treatment is useful when sunscreen lotion hasn't been applied as carefully as it should be.

Glossary

BELAY – to hold or secure a rope while another climbs. Best done with the assistance of a belay device; alternately, with a section of rope wrapped around the waist (belaying should only be attempted by those who've been instructed in proper technique).

BOLTS (for climbing) – metal brackets that a lead climber can clip into for protection or assistance. The bolt itself is drilled and sometimes glued into rock, and then fitted with a hanger.

CAIRN – a pile of rocks marking a hiking route, or high point such as a ridge or mountain summit.

CHIMNEY (rock) – a narrow cleft between at least two rock walls, often steep but relatively easy to ascend with proper climbing technique.

CROSS COUNTRY BIKING – mountain biking over rolling or level terrain. Cross country rides may involve steep uphill climbs and even steeper descents, but more often endeavors to traverse a piece of ground.

DOWNHILL RIDING – often involves the assistance of a vehicle or lift to reach a certain height before one hops into the saddle.

FIN (SANDSTONE) – A flat, thin and often upturned slab of sandstone, eroded over time into this particular shape. Fins commonly give rise to rock "windows"; literally openings in the middle of rock slabs that can reach considerable width and height.

LEAD CLIMBING – as opposed to seconding, the lead climber establishes a climbing rope for others to follow. Normally he/she risks the greatest chance of a fall.

LEAD PROTECTION – literally, protection for a leader to guard against serious falls while climbing above partner(s).

SCRAMBLE – is more difficult and adventuresome than hiking, but less so than climbing or mountaineering. Scrambling often involves using hands, as well as feet, to surmount obstacles or to follow a route. The Southwest is full of easy scrambles and more difficult ROPED SCRAMBLES, where a rope is recommended for reasons of safety.

SCREE – refers to an accumulation of rocks from gravel to small boulder size. Scree is found throughout the Southwest, covering slopes of moderate to fairly steep gradients. It can be fun and relatively easy to descend, but is notoriously difficult to climb over.

SWITCHBACK – a zig-zag trail or road routing. Switchbacks are usually encountered on steep slopes to reduce grade, or to allow passage over landscape features – such as cliffs – that would otherwise prove difficult to ascend, or descend.

TALUS – like SCREE, but bigger in size. Generally not as easy or as much fun to descend as its smaller brethren.

WASH – A sandy or gravelly low-lying bed that remains dry except during or immediately after a rainstorm. Washes are often interesting places for wildlife viewing, and may offer the best routing through terrain in lieu of a trail, but they should be avoided if any danger of flash floods exist.

APPENDIX

Health and Safety Contacts

The following hospitals are located closest to the "base" communities listed.

Joshua Tree:
Hi-Desert Medical Center
6601 White Feather Road,
Joshua Tree, California
760-366-3711

Lone Pine:
Southern Inyo Hospital
501 East Locus Street,
Lone Pine, California
760-876-5501

Bishop:
Northern Inyo Hospital
150 Pioneer Lane,
Bishop, California
760-873-5811

Springdale:
Dixie Regional Medical Center (45 miles from Springdale)
544 South 400 East,
St. George, Utah
435-688-4000

Zion Canyon Medical Clinic (only open part-time during the winter months)
120 Lion Boulevard,
Springdale, Utah
435-772-3226

Kanab:
Kane County Hospital
355 S. Main Street,
Kanab, Utah
435-644-5811

Moab:
Allen Memorial Hospital
719 West 400 North,
Moab, Utah
435-259-7191

Sedona:
Flagstaff Medical Center (a full-service hospital 30 miles away)
1200 N. Beaver Street,
Flagstaff, Arizona
928-779-3366

Verde Valley Medical Center (a full-service hospital 17.5 miles away)
269 S. Candy Lane,
Cottonwood, Arizona
928-639-6000

Sedona Medical Center (for emergency and outpatient care)

3700 W. Highway 89A,
Sedona, Arizona
928-204-3000

Ajo:
Desert Senita Community
Health Center (an outpatient
clinic with emergency facilities open on weekdays only)
410 Malacate Street,
Ajo, Arizona
520-387-5651

Tucson Medical Center (74
miles from Ajo)
1501 N. Campbell Avenue,
Tucson, Arizona
520-694-0111

Santa Fe:
St. Vincent Regional Medical
Center
455 St. Michael's Drive,
Santa Fe, New Mexico
505-983-3361

Alamogordo:
Gerald Champion Regional
Medical Center
2669 Scenic Drive,
Alamogordo, New Mexico
505-439-6100

Carlsbad:
Carlsbad Medical Center
2430 West Pierce,
Carlsbad, New Mexico
505-887-4100

Other Emergency Phone Numbers:

F = Fire
P = Police
A = Ambulance

The following are all emergency back-up numbers.
Dialing "911" will allow you
to contact fire, police or
ambulance services in any of
the base communities.

Joshua Tree/Twentynine Palms:
(F) 760-367-7524
(P) 760-367-9546
(A) 760-366-8474

Bishop/Lone Pine:
(F) 760-876-4826
(P) 760-873-5866
(A) 760-876-4826

Springdale:
(F) 911
(P) 911
(A) 911

Kanab:
(F) 435-644-2718
(P) 435-644-5854
(A) 435-644-2718

Moab:
(F) 435-259-5557
(P) 435-259-8938
(A) 435-259-5557

Sedona:
(F) 928-282-6800
(P) 928-282-3100
(A) 928-282-6800

Ajo:
(F) 911
(P) 911
(A) 911

Santa Fe:
(F) 505-428-3710
(P) 505-955-5144
(A) 505-955-5144

Alamogordo:
(F) 911
(P) 505-439-4300
(A) 911

Carlsbad:
(F) 911
(P) 911
(A) 911

Park Emergencies

Joshua Tree/Twentynine Palms:

Joshua Tree National Park:
760-367-5500

Bishop/Lone Pine:
Mount Whitney Ranger Station: 760-876-6200

Kanab or Springdale:
Zion Park Ranger Station:
435-772-3256

Sedona:
Red Rock State Park: 928-282-6907

Moab:
Canyonlands National Park:
435-719-2313 or 435-259-4351

Arches National Park:
435-259-8161

Ajo:
Organ Pipe Cactus National Monument: 520-387-6849

Weather Information

From flash floods in slot canyons to freak hailstorms, weather conditions in the Southwest can change rapidly. For this reason, we recommend consulting the National Weather Service's reports at www.weather.gov. They are up-to-date and reliable (at least as much as any forecast can be).

Another useful website for weather forecasts and current weather conditions is at www.americansouthwest.net In addition to listing weather conditions in particular parks, this site also contains links to Weather Underground, The Weather Channel and CNN.

Equipment and Clothing

Joshua Tree/ Twentynine Palms:

Coyote Corner

Climbing and camping gear rentals. The store even has hot showers for that always welcome chance to freshen up.
6535 Park Boulevard (in Joshua Tree)
Phone: 760-366-9673

Nomad Ventures

A friendly gear shop offering a good selection of outdoor equipment, climbing gear and guides.
61795 29 Palms Highway (across from Coyote Corner in Joshua Tree).
Phone: 760-366-4684

Cottonwood Camping & Surplus

General camping supplies.
6376 Adobe Road (in Twentynine Palms)
Phone: 619-367-9505

Springdale:

Zion Cycles

This shop prides itself on providing rental bikes and equipment for families. Staff here will be able to point you towards trails that best suit your kids' abilities and also provide up-to-date advice on trail conditions. Free parking is available at the shop, so you can enjoy your ride worry-free. If you're bringing your own bikes and live in the continental U.S.,

Zion Cycles can arrange to assemble them and store the bike cases, and then repack the bikes and ship them back to your home address.
868 Zion Park Boulevard
Phone: 435-772-0400

Springdale Cycles and Tours

This shop offers tours of Zion National Park as well as half-day, full-day and multi-day rentals. The staff request that you call ahead to ensure that bike rentals are available.
1458 Zion Park Boulevard
Phone: 435-772-0575

Zion Rock and Mountain Guides

Canyoneering, climbing, hiking and backpacking gear for all ages are available at this shop. The friendly and well-informed staff can tell you exactly what you'll need for a trek up Zion's slot canyons or for hikes elsewhere in the park. In addition to gear sales, equipment rentals and information, this shop offers guide services, instruction courses and a hiker's trailhead shuttle service. They're also happy to customize arrangements for families.
1458 Zion Park Boulevard
Phone: 435-772-3303

Kanab:

Willow Canyon Outdoor Gear

This store offers hiking gear that ranges from packs and boots to topographical maps and camping food. Mom and dad can also get a good espresso here!
263 S. 100 East Kanab
Phone: 435-644-8884

Canyon Rim Adventures

This company's primary focus is on providing guided tours through the Grand Canyon (North Rim) and into the Kaibab National Forest. You can rent camping, hiking and backpacking equipment, as well as mountain bikes.

520 S 475 East Kanab
Phone: 435-644-8512

Moab:

Gearheads

Among many other things, this store has the largest selection of climbing gear in Moab. Accessories are available for biking, hiking, climbing, boating and off-roading. A nice feature of this store is the large water filtration station, where customers can fill up with as much free water as they want — no strings attached! There's also a great selection of power snacks, such as Clif Bars.

471 South Main Street (in the Desert Plaza)
Phone: 435-259-4327

Red Rock Outfitters

This store can outfit you with just about anything. If you've chosen to take a tour with a local company (e.g. a rafting trip with the Moab Adventure Center), this store can provide you with a packing list indicating all the necessary supplies. Check out the very useful website (www.redrockoutfitters.com) to check out everything that's available.

225 South Main Street
Phone: 435-259-9941

Rim Cyclery

This place has a world-famous reputation for mountain bike rentals, sales and service and is Moab's oldest bike and outdoor gear store. Rim Cyclery's experienced mechanics can give you excellent advice on trails, bike pur-

chases, repairs or gear. The store sells all the most popular brands of camping gear, climbing gear, packs and clothing. Reservations are recommended for bike and equipment rentals.

497 North Main Street
Phone: 435-259-7448

Poison Spider Bicycles

Don't let the name scare you away from this all-purpose shop. Although Poison Spider specializes in bike rentals, sales and servicing, it also sells and rents outdoor clothing and backcountry gear. It has lots of maps and guides available, too. There's a nice selection of kid's bikes for rent, as well as Burley bike trailers. Reservations for gear rentals are recommended, since Poison Spider can get quite busy (especially during the high season). The owners of Poison Spider have been riding in Moab since the '80s, so they know just the right trails for you and the kids to try.

497 North Main Street
Phone: 435-259-7882

Sedona:

Sedona Sports

This place bills itself as "Sedona's Premier Outdoor Outfitter" — and for good reason. The equipment ranges from sunglasses to hiking shoes. Rental gear includes: mountain bikes, GPS units, binoculars, walking sticks, baby carrier packs and jogging strollers.

251 Highway 179 (Creekside Plaza)
Phone: 928-282-1317

Bike and Bean

This is probably Sedona's best bike shop (although it's actually located in nearby Oak Creek), with good rental choices for kids. It's conveniently located just across the street from some excellent family-friendly trails on red rock.

6020 Highway 179 (in the village of Oak Creek)

Phone: 928-284-0210

Absolute Bikes

Absolute Bikes is located close to Bike and Bean. The store stocks bicycles, bike parts, accessories and clothing for all types of riders (from hardcore enthusiasts to novices) and gear that covers mountain, road and BMX biking.

There's a good selection of supplies for kids, too.

6101 Highway 179, Suite C (in the village of Oak Creek)

Phone: 928-284-1242

Canyon Outfitters

This is Sedona's largest and most complete outdoor store for hiking, camping, backpacking and climbing clothing and gear. There's also a large selection of hydration packs.

2701 West Highway 89A

Phone: 928-282-5293

Traveling Websites

Following is a list of useful websites we've discovered while preparing to travel with our kids. It is, of course, partial at best:

www.journeyswithkids.com

OK, we're biased! Our website does more than just encourage readers to pick up our books though. It also offers vital information on destinations other than those covered in our books, supports dialogue between traveling parents, and will soon host games to keep young ones entertained while on the road.

www.adventuringwithchildren.com

www.atmtravel.co.uk

www.familyadventures.com

www.familyonboard.com

www.familytravelfiles.com

www.familytravelforum.com

www.familytravelnetwork.com

www.kidsholidaysonline.com

www.lonelyplanet.com

www.nationalgeographic.com\kids

www.singleparenttravel.net

www.travelforkids.com

www.travellanguages.com/travel

www.takethekidstravelling.com

ADVENTURING IN ITALY

Our family of five has toured over 35 countries. Inspiration, adventure and excitement have highlighted our every adventure. So it is with no small endorsement when we say Italy is our favorite travel destination.

So what makes Italy so special?

Italy combines all the best things in life and furnishes them with grace and style. With this guidebook in hand, chances are, you and your family will agree with us.

Start with the food. Kids (and adults!) rejoice: pizza, pasta, fresh produce and gelati are as diverse as they are delicious. The prosecco, and expresso - for mom and dad – magnifico!

Italians exude as much gusto in person as they do in the culinary arts. People are friendly with kids and towards families. Italians know how to have fun, and treasure comradely spirit and enthusiasm in others.

Italy's history is steeped in both modernity and antiquity. A center of Western Civilization, Italy's sculpture, philosophy and architecture spans the time of Christ through medieval and renaissance times. Today, Italy's crumbling ruins, hilltop castles and exquisite works of art are sure to excite and absorb youngsters and adults.

Families will find Italy's modern culture just as fascinating. The Italian zest for sports in general – and football (soccer) in particular – is infectious. Modern design also inspires: Ferrari, Lamborghini, Prada and Gucci.

Italians enthusiastically embrace every activity their rich and varied topography allows. From cliff diving along the sun-soaked Tyrrhenian coastline; to cliff climbing the rock of the Dolomites; and from biking through rolling Tuscan countryside; to relaxing on the velvet beaches of the Adriatic. The Italian mindset is very much devoted to recreation.

Perhaps this is what we find most captivating about Italy. There are so many activities and sights. During a two-week vacation, you and your kids can build sand castles, swim through crystalline waters, sail lively seas, mountain bike, hike, climb and ascend via ferratas.

Buon appettito and buon viaggio!

On bookstore shelves in 2007

FAVORITE BEACH DESTINATIONS

Life is a beach. Especially when you're a kid. A beach environment is one of nature's greatest endowments and is packed with educational opportunities on shore and beneath the waves. A sunny beach is also hard to beat for adult play and relaxation.

Ideally suited to families having fun and exploring together, the world's beaches have provided my family among their most memorable vacations. And this is why I chose to write this book.

How does a beach become a "favorite?" It must allow for a relaxing time with children, yet must also offer more than a simple beach "getaway", such as unique cultural attributes; feature great beauty and captivating wildlife; or offer a fantastic range of activities. Some of the beaches we have chosen to highlight combine all three.

Favorites include several of the world's most scenic beaches as well as some that are perhaps not quite as visually stunning. But all are beautiful in their own ways.

Featured are 11 beach destinations. They include three from the Americas (Mexico's Los Cabos and Mayan Riviera, as well as Costa Rica); three from the Pacific region (Kauai, Tahiti and the Cook Islands); three from Africa (Cape Town, the Seychelles and Egypt's Red Sea); and two from Asia (Thailand and Bali).

You probably already have a list of beach favorites. Enjoy ours. This guide will help you build a greater appreciation and appetite for exploring the sand and surf at beaches around the world.

On bookstore shelves in 2007

IBERIA MEETS AFRICA

Where the Iberian Peninsula and Africa meets is one of the world's most intriguing places. Warm and colourful the area is legendary, making it especially well suited to family adventure travel.

Hundreds of miles of beach and surf along the Costa Blanca, Costa del Sol and Portuguese Algarve provide an endless playground for exploration on (bare) foot.

Venture inland and you and your children will walk the trails of the Sierra Nevada Range, tracing the steps of the badoleros - Robin Hood-like thieves who invaded hillside villages.

Be exposed to a regional culture inspired by a now-receded wave of Moorish occupiers and now-predominant Catholic custom. Nearby castles and palaces - like the Alhambra in Granada, and Seville's Alcazar - showcase minarets and Muslim mosaics, or towering crucifixes and imagery of Mary and Christ.

Bring to life the complex history and the often-tenuous relation between Islam and Christianity. Explore a vivid history that will certainly inspire questions from your children.

This delta of cultures manifests in Southern Iberian cuisine. In Portugal's Algarve region, figs and almonds, common to Middle Eastern dishes, have been integrated in local specialties. Andalucia's tapas restaurants are a legacy of the 781-year Moorish history.

This guide suggests ways to get the most from your family's visit to the Iberian region. Along with tips on the best places to beach comb, rock climb, mountain bike and ride horseback, essential pointers for in-depth cultural exploration of castles, ruins and other monuments is provided. Also, the guide will advise on visiting nearby Morocco with kids, suggesting best places and activities while balancing issues of health and safety.

On bookstore shelves by 2007